D0093900

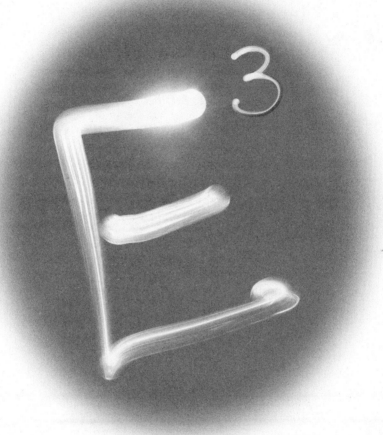

ALSO BY PAM GROUT

Jumpstart Your Metabolism:
How to Lose Weight by Changing the Way You Breathe

Art and Soul: 156 Ways to Free Your Creative Spirit

Living Big: Embrace Your Passion and
Leap into an Extraordinary Life

Kansas Curiosities: Quirky Characters,
Roadside Oddities & Other Offbeat Stuff

Colorado Curiosities: Quirky Characters,
Roadside Oddities & Other Offbeat Stuff

Girlfriend Getaways: You Go, Girl, and I'll Go, Too

You Know You're in Kansas When: 101 Quintessential Places,
People, Events, Customs, Lingo and Eats of the Sunflower State

Recycle This Book: And 72½ Even Better
Ways to Save "Yo Momma" Earth

God Doesn't Have Bad Hair Days

100 Best Vacations to Enrich Your Life

100 Best Worldwide Vacations to Enrich Your Life

100 Best Volunteer Vacations to Enrich Your Life

E-Squared: Nine Do-It-Yourself Energy Experiments
That Prove Your Thoughts Create Your Reality*

*Available from Hay House

Please visit:

Hay House USA: www.hayhouse.com®
Hay House Australia: www.hayhouse.com.au
Hay House UK: www.hayhouse.co.uk
Hay House South Africa: www.hayhouse.co.za
Hay House India: www.hayhouse.co.in

NINE MORE ENERGY EXPERIMENTS THAT PROVE MANIFESTING MAGIC AND MIRACLES IS YOUR FULL-TIME GIG

PAM GROUT

HAY HOUSE, INC.
Carlsbad, California • New York City
London • Sydney • Johannesburg
Vancouver • Hong Kong • New Delhi

Published and distributed in the United States by: Hay House, Inc.: www .hayhouse.com® • *Published and distributed in Australia by:* Hay House Australia Pty. Ltd.: www.hayhouse.com.au • *Published and distributed in the United Kingdom by:* Hay House UK, Ltd.: www.hayhouse.co.uk • *Published and distributed in the Republic of South Africa by:* Hay House SA (Pty), Ltd.: www.hayhouse.co.za • *Distributed in Canada by:* Raincoas Books: www .raincoast.com • *Published in India by:* Hay House Publishers India: www .hayhouse.co.in

Cover design: Amy Rose Grigoriou   *Interior design:* Pamela Homan

Library of Congress Cataloging-in-Publication Data

Grout, Pam.
  E-cubed : nine more energy experiments that prove manifesting magic and miracles is your full-time gig / Pam Grout. -- 1st edition.
    pages cm
  ISBN 978-1-4019-4543-5 (paperback)
  1. Self-actualization (Psychology) 2. New Thought. 3. Spiritual life. I. Title.
  BF637.S4G7743 2014
  158.1--dc23
                                    2014020093

Tradepaper ISBN: 978-1-4019-4543-5
Digital ISBN: 978-1-4019-4685-2

10 9 8 7 6 5 4 3 2 1
1st edition, September 2014

SUSTAINABLE FORESTRY INITIATIVE
Certified Chain of Custody
Promoting Sustainable Forestry
www.sfiprogram.org
SFI-01268
SFI label applies to the text stock

Printed in the United States of America

For Spelling Bee Rachael,
whose enormous spirit is far too wise,
generous, and joyously irreverent for this
limited physical plane.*

*Rachael Marie Sheridan
(November 28, 1974–February 24, 2014)

CONTENTS

FOREWORD

As a self-proclaimed miracle worker, I get super-psyched to practice the power of positive intention in everything I do. When I got my hands on Pam Grout's book *E-Squared*, I knew right away I'd been given a gift—the gift of reinforcing my faith in the power of the universe. In an early chapter of *E-Squared*, Pam invites us to try an experiment in which we ask the universe to give us a blessing. She emphasizes that we must pay attention over the next 48 hours to see what comes our way. We must look closely for the little wink from the universe that reminds us we're being guided.

Thirty-eight hours into my experiment, I received my blessing. I was in Toronto speaking at one of Hay House's conferences. That day I gave one of my greatest talks. I felt the energy of the room elevate, and I experienced an intimate connection with an audience of more than 4,000 people. Immediately after my talk, I went to the green room to pack up my bags and rush to the airport. It was the final day of the conference, so most of the other speakers had already left or were on their way out. There were only three of us left in the room. As I put on my coat to walk out the door, a man in the room picked up something off a table and said, "Gabby, I found this and I'm not sure why, but I know it's for you." He handed me a small angel wing charm that had *Believe* printed on the back.

In that moment I knew I'd received my blessing from the universe. The actual wing was particularly meaningful to me because I often feel the presence of angels around me, and the universe speaks to us in ways that are relevant to our core beliefs. Not only was the angel wing meaningful, but what also made an impact was the word *Believe.* When I received this gift from the universe, I happened to be in the first week of a new book launch. I was struggling to find faith that everything would work out the way I'd planned. This angel message to believe was everything I needed to accept that I was on the right track. Pam's experiment reminded me that the universe shows up when we need it most.

Moments like this are not foreign to me, though they always make me smile. I have dedicated my life to believing in the power of our energy and intentions, and I'm a long-time student of metaphysics and the law of attraction. Even still, I sometimes forget just how deeply we're being guided and how the universe is always waiting for us to simply pay attention. Our work as spiritual students is to commit to a journey of unlearning fear and remembering miracles. And Pam Grout is the perfect teacher for sharpening our capacity to remember.

What I admire most about Pam is her commitment to guiding people to shift their perceptions and heighten their faith. She is a master manifestor and is living proof of everything that she teaches. In her new book, *E-Cubed,* she takes our miracle mind-sets to a whole new level. Whether you're experienced at manifesting or totally new to the practice, *E-Cubed* is a must-have for strengthening your belief in the power of positive intention. Living this way takes practice (most of us are stuck in fear in so many subtle ways that we have a lot of unlearning to do), and that's what *E-Cubed* and Pam offer. The best part is her exercises and experiments are not only really powerful, but they're easy to learn and a lot of fun. When we embrace the natural order of the law of attraction, we begin to accept that we have the power to co-create our reality. This is when life gets really groovy. Using the power of our thoughts and intentions to create a life we love is an artful craft. It's a thrill to use our greatest untapped resource: our thoughts and energy.

The *only* reason you're not aware of this nonstop stream of blessings and miracles is because you're looking in the wrong places. With just a little willingness and awareness, it's amazing what can happen. As Wayne Dyer often says, you've got to believe it to see it.

Through eye-opening experiments, *E-Cubed* gives us an engaging way to practice staying in the flow of abundance and synchronicity. So enjoy the process, surrender to Pam's guidance, and expect miracles!

— Gabrielle Bernstein
New York Times best-selling author of *Miracles Now*

PREFACE

Before I became a serious student of *A Course in Miracles,* I was the last person anyone would have picked out of a police lineup as "most likely to succeed."

At the time, my boyfriend, the last in a long series of boyfriends, had kicked me out of the house we shared in rural Connecticut.

To top it off, I was seven months pregnant, obviously unmarried, and had nary a clue where to go. Even worse, it was mid-July and the air conditioner in the little blue Toyota in which I'd stuffed most of my earthly possessions was on the fritz. Temperatures averaged 100 degrees as I set out across the country, big as a house, pointed in the general direction of Breckenridge, Colorado.

Clearly, something needed to change.

A Course in Miracles, a self-study program in spiritual psychology that I began to follow in earnest, had the audacity to suggest that I was responsible for my train wreck of a life. It implied that if I would simply let go of all my mad fixations, my "he done me wrong" blockages, and all the other clutter I'd picked up about the way the world works, I could actually be happy. It suggested that the only reason I wasn't experiencing big-ass love and swimming in perpetual abundance was because my consciousness was on red alert. My thoughts viewed the world as my sworn enemy.

In short, it challenged the very foundation of my life.

I didn't let go without a fight.

My conversations with JC and the Holy S, as I began to call my *Course* comrades, went something like this:

> **Me:** "But what about all my problems? Shouldn't I analyze and fix them?"
>
> "Let go!" the *Course* seemed to suggest.
>
> **Me:** "But what about good and evil, right and wrong?"
>
> "Resign now as your own teacher," it clearly advised.
>
> **Me:** "But . . . but . . ."

Slowly, inch by inch, I gave up the reins to my beliefs and old mental constructs. It began to occur to me that if reality was my doing, if it was me creating the ongoing disaster, I might also have the power to create a life I could enjoy. The *Course*, in fact, pulled no punches, going so far as to guarantee that "perfect peace and perfect joy" are my inheritance. All I had to do was give up my belief in deprivation and lack.

> "But that's so hard," I whined.
>
> "It's not hard," the *Course* said. "It's your natural state. It's just *very* different than the way most people think."

I also learned from the *Course* that the tall blonde chick I see every day in the mirror isn't really me. The depressed pregnant woman driving the blue Toyota cross-country was nothing but a false identity I'd been taught to assume by a world that worships separation and limitations.

In fact, by focusing in on that little "self," I completely missed my connection to this other thing, this bigger thing that many call God.

I had completely imprisoned myself by zeroing in on this rickety body that—no matter how many face creams I used, no matter how many downward-facing dogs I did, no matter how many Wayne Dyer books I read (and I read a lot)—was never going to be good enough.

And that's what this book is about: Taking the wrecking ball to mental constructs that have imprisoned us for far too long. Taking the focus off the limited self we see in the mirror and putting it on the glorious field of potentiality (the FP) that allows us to connect to all that is.

I know bookstores will likely catalog this book under the self-help banner, and that's okay. But truth be told, *E-Cubed* is really about *not* helping yourself. About *not* making your own decisions. About *not* assuming you know best.

It's about letting go—giving up old mental constructs and surrendering to the all-loving, all-powerful energy force that's bigger, bolder, brighter, and, yes, stranger than anything you've yet seen. This Sacred Buzz is life itself. Life, which—no matter how many walls we erect, no matter how seriously we screw up—is always there waiting with arms open wide.

PART I

BAZINGA!

*"Under all the senseless thoughts and mad ideas
with which you have cluttered up your mind
are the thoughts that you thought
with God* in the beginning."*
— A COURSE IN MIRACLES

* Aka the field of infinite potentiality, the FP, the Universe,
Divine Spirit, the Dude, Quantum Fred**

** Moniker provided by my new friend Colette Baron-Reid

CHAPTER ONE

HOUSTON, WE HAVE A PROBLEM

"Just look at us. Everything is backwards, everything is upside down. Religion destroys spirituality, doctors destroy health and governments destroy freedom."

— MICHAEL ELLNER, PRESIDENT OF HEAL,
A NOT-FOR-PROFIT HEALTH EDUCATION ASSOCIATION

I know what you're thinking. Your copy of this book is messed up. The text is printed upside down . . . or is it backward? Maybe you're chuckling to yourself, wondering whose head is going to roll—the typesetter or the printer or maybe even your friendly bookstore associate?

So let me propose a speedy détente, right here in the third paragraph. This page was printed upside down on purpose. I requested it that way because I WANT. TO. MAKE. A. POINT.

I want to warn you straightaway that your worldview, should you continue to read this weird, upside-down book, is about to be turned on its pointy little head. If you thought Linda Blair's head spun in *The Exorcist,* well, baby, get ready for some pea-green soup.

If you're reading this book on the subway or in a coffee shop and worried that people are wondering, *Hey, who's the illiterate idiot holding his book upside down?* I have but two things to say.

1. It matters not what anybody else thinks. That's part of your old-school conditioning that I encourage you to drop-kick to the nearest curb. In fact, if you *really* want to make an impression, smile deviously and pump your fists in the air every time you turn a page. The more you hold on to what you want to think (and make no mistake—you get to decide) and the less you buy into what everybody else thinks, the faster you can step into your highest good.

2. The only thing that matters is what *you* think. And I mean that quite literally. What you think is what you get. And this book, above all else, is about bettering, to use a Dr. Seuss word, your thinking. It's about upgrading your consciousness. About becoming an early adopter of Worldview 2.0. Eventually, everybody's going to get the new reality anyway. So why wait?

So What Exactly Is Worldview 2.0?

> *"[Accept] but the joyous as the truth."*
> — *A Course in Miracles*

In a nutshell, this new and improved worldview is the exact opposite—or the upside-down version—of everything you think you know now.

4

It has two main principles:

1. The energetic world, the world you can't see, touch, taste, or smell, is the foundation on which all else rests. It's the building block—the supreme cheese—that forms everything. Scientists discovered this matrix of energy (often called The Field) about a century ago, but because it's so mind-blowing and opens up so many new doors, very few of us have yet fully employed its power.

Most of us, 100 years later, are still focused on the material world, which is a little like rooting for Wile E. Coyote. Despite all his elaborate schemes and complex contraptions, that sorry ole coyote is never going to catch the Roadrunner. And our stubbornness (*beep-beep!*) in believing that the cut-and-dried, machinelike world is the be-all and end-all keeps us in spiritual diapers.

The spiritual world, the world that most of us can't see, connects us to an unlimited, enormous consciousness with no edges, no boundaries, and no limits to what it can create.

2. Everybody gets a happy ending. Everything in the nonphysical world is cooperative, user-friendly, and win-win. In fact, the real world, without the blinders, is nothing like you think. It's nothing like the movie set you manufactured to serve as "your reality." No matter how it may appear to the naked eye, life in its pure, unadulterated form (without our "life sucks and then you die" consciousness laid over it) is a bubbling cauldron of possibility, composed of pure, perfect love.

The very fact that we still see heartache, limitations, and death is proof that we do not understand reality at all. We focus in on a very narrow band of experience, completely denying the many dimensions beyond the five physical senses.

5

Our ignorance has erected a worldview based solely on problems, on fear, on protecting ourselves from all the things that *could* go wrong. It has led us to separate ourselves from the whole and to believe that this, this limited viewfinder filled with individual beings, is what we have to work with.

Consequently, we use our enormous, inexhaustible consciousness to scope out escape routes. Every moment we waste on worst-case scenarios undermines our ability to create the true and the beautiful. Every moment we spend worrying erects a block between us and all the signs and opportunities and, yes, blatant love that is here for the sole purpose of our enjoyment. We've flipped the map of Truth with "facts" from our negative orientation. When negativity emerges (and it *will*, because our consciousness, no matter how altered and off-base it may be, is powerful), we feel validated. We smirk and think, *See, told you so.*

But as you'll learn in Worldview 2.0, the dominant "life sucks and then you die" paradigm is nothing but a fictional story, a made-up pack of lies we've been telling ourselves for the last . . . I don't know . . . 40,000 years?

We're trained from a very early age to put on a pair of gray-colored glasses and look at the world through the lens of defeat and pain. We get brownie points for finding problems. Expecting the good in life and assuming the best outcome sounds dangerously like "not facing up to reality." There is a bias against too much optimism and happiness.

Even therapists, who purport to brighten our lives, encourage us to dig up old baggage and peek at creaky skeletons lurking in our subconscious closets. They pat us on the back for noticing where we're stuck, for paying attention to how we are suffering.

But it's not any more true than all those zombie movies that are so popular right now.

How Does Your Mental Garden Grow?

"Reality is up for grabs."

— MELISSA JOY, PRESIDENT OF MATRIX ENERGETICS

In Worldview 2.0, you'll quickly come to realize that life is meant to be approached with exuberance and joy, and that "Follow your bliss" is not an empty platitude for a bumper sticker, but rather a reasonable plan of action for your life. If that's not the way your life is playing out, then something, as Emmy Award–winning newscaster Andy Cordan likes to say, is messed up. If magic isn't happening to you on a daily basis—if you're not waking up every morning with passion and zest—you're living in a horror picture that you concocted to entertain yourself.

And that's what *E-Cubed* intends to prove. That the old way of thinking has run its course and that a higher reality is pushing its way in. All we have to do is let go of the drama and get it that the zombie movie we believe is reality is boring, redundant, and completely unnecessary.

So, in this book, I'm going to ask you to put Worldview 1.0 on pause while you conduct the nine experiments in Part II. I'd like to suggest, at least for the 30 days it takes to try them on for size, that you suspend your beliefs, become willing to set aside certainty and absolutes.

In *E-Squared,* the book that inspired this one, I pointed out that energy transmits itself into whatever structure our consciousness sets up. Without the squaring action of our thoughts and beliefs, the world remains in a timeless, spaceless state of ever-changing possibilities. If our limited perceptions create an energy structure negating the inexhaustible substance in which we live, we end up with a small, often-times-scary reality. Because we identify so deeply with this limited reality, it seems very real to us. It seems as if we have no choice. We certainly don't recognize that it's our doing. Negativity, slyly disguised as "reality," has become a construct that, like Harry Potter's magical cloak, is now invisible to us.

In *E-Squared,* I encouraged readers to begin viewing the world through the eyes of *What could go right?* instead of the more popular paradigm, *What could go wrong? E-Squared* provided the training wheels to this radical new paradigm. In *E-Cubed,* we're ready to fly.

Quantum Dizziness

"We can no longer consider ourselves merely onlookers who have no effect on the world that we're observing. . . . The very act of observation is an act of creation."
— JOHN WHEELER, AMERICAN
THEORETICAL PHYSICIST

We live in a quantum age where people can instantaneously text each other across the planet, repair detached retinas with nothing but laser beams, and use little handheld devices to get money-saving Groupons. Yet, in our thinking, in our applications of these new truths, we're lagging sorely behind. We're still using Industrial Age thinking. We're not using the incredible power of our consciousness. Our consciousness, which can and does create worlds.

We're more than a century into this new quantum reality, and we've barely budged in our thinking. We haven't even begun to use these startling new processes in our personal lives. Instead, we invest our thoughts—our power, if you will—in victimhood, in this idea that life happens *to* us. This warped view of reality wouldn't be an issue if our thoughts were mere puffs of smoke, blown away by the next breeze.

But our thoughts are insanely powerful.

Like radio signals, our thoughts broadcast our beliefs and expectations out into the quantum field (or what I like to call the field of potentiality, the FP) and bring back into our lives an exact vibrational match. Quantum physicists have proven that it's impossible for us to look at anything without impacting the thing we're looking at. It's called the *observer effect,* and while it wreaks havoc on everything we thought we knew, it's actually quite exciting. Because it means:

1. We're not stuck with the 3-D reality we think is "it."

2. We're not helpless victims.

3. And there's a whole cheerleading squad of multidimensions just waiting for us to get with the program.

What we now know is that everything we think is an objective world "out there" is nothing but a reflection of what exists in here. And by "in here" I mean the consciousness that is doing the observing.

You've heard this before, but when your thoughts center on joy, love, and peace, your life experience will be one of joy, love, and peace. But when your consciousness stays tuned to radio station K-FKD—the dominant soundtrack of our culture, the soundtrack of pain and woe—you get . . . do I really have to say it?

Look What Your Thoughts Drug In

"The separated ones have invented many 'cures' for what they believe to be 'the ills of the world.' But the one thing they do not do is to question the reality of the problem."
— A COURSE IN MIRACLES

9

Our consciousness is like the house cat that proudly brings back to the front doorstep the squirrel or wren upon which he greedily pounced. It's his way of saying, *Hey, inferior owner of mine, look what I brought you.*

It's totally cool that your thoughts wield this kind of influence. It means that you and a relatively active imagination can create just about anything you desire. By sending your thoughts out into the quantum field as scouts, they bring back all sorts of riches. Just ask the readers of *E-Squared,* whose expanding consciousness manifested everything from an appearance on *Dr. Oz* to six Tesla roadsters to offers for literary representation from William Morris, Creative Artists Agency, ICM Partners, and United Talent Agency.

The downside of your Lewis and Clark thoughts is that when your view of the world and yourself and everything in between is swayed so heavily by the past—on what happened yesterday, on a bunch of outdated, old-school paradigms touting lack, limitation, and nasal buildup—your thoughts, like the house cat, drag in a lot of squished-squirrel surprise.

Instead of enjoying the world's bounty, instead of seeing every day as a brand new opportunity to dance the joy soul boogie, your thoughts bring back the same old rotten, lice-ridden squished-squirrel soup.

I want to stamp my foot and say, "Stop that!" But instead I've written this book.

It's Just How We Roll

"Let's take it higher, baby."
— TAMA KIEVES, FORMER LAWYER AND
CURRENT LIFE COACH

The true Reality (that we're all one, that the world is abundant and strangely accommodating, and that love is the final answer) is starting to emerge in the hearts and minds of individuals all over the planet, individuals who are standing up and proclaiming, "This can't be right. There has *got* to be a better way!"

The way I see it, there are just two things we need to know:

1. The universe has our back.

2. Everything is going to turn out okay.

That's 12 freaking words. Everything else is just a big ruse that we, in our misguided thoughts, sent scouts out to retrieve from the field of infinite potentiality. So, yes, I'm offering nine more energy experiments in this book. Over-achievers will even be challenged to turn water into a glass of their favorite Cabernet. But mostly, this book is about sending the scouts (aka your beliefs, those all-powerful vibrating waves) in search of different things—to "get it" that joy is your natural state and should be your guiding light on this earthly journey. Having fun and feeling good is your purpose. That's why you're here. That's the secret to everything.

If you've followed my blog (and if you haven't, I have a very important question: *Why not? . . .* you are hereby invited to come and join the fun—for newbies, it's www.pamgrout .com), you probably know that I wrote *E-Squared* nine years ago. It came out, under a different title, about the same time as the movie *The Secret,* way before the book and the resulting clones that followed. But instead of capturing the public's imagination as I assumed it would, it took a nosedive into the great sea of literary has-beens, quickly going out of print. I waved a white flag, got busy writing three travel books for *National Geographic,* and didn't spend too much time obsessing. Okay, a little bit of time.

A couple of years ago, I dusted it off, gave it a new title, and sent it off to Hay House, a publisher that specializes in these kinds of books. And as you may have heard, *E-Squared* became an international sensation. Both books, although with different titles, are essentially the same. Why did one trip on the way to the dance floor and the other waltz off into international stardom?

Here's what I think. The title *E-Squared* may be a tad more compelling than *God Doesn't Have Bad Hair Days*. And, yes, the timing is right (consciousness evolving and all that), but I truly believe the most important variable is that my vibration changed; I upgraded my consciousness. Like Hans and Franz from *Saturday Night Live,* I said to my joy channels, "I'm going to pump you up."

I got rid of a lot of the negative twigs that were gunking up the pipes. This will sound rather controversial, but I became committed to living in constant joy. I began noticing all the blessings in my life that, as I've also said on my blog, now stalk me like Freddy Krueger.

And as I became happy, my external world, which is nothing but the projector of my internal thoughts, began showing a different picture.

In retrospect, I should have seen it coming.

CHAPTER TWO

SPANX FOR THE MEMORY

*"Traditional human power structures and their reign of
darkness are about to be rendered obsolete."*
— BUCKMINSTER FULLER, AMERICAN FUTURIST

One of my favorite stories is about a four-year-old boy
who kept pestering his parents for some "alone time" with his
newborn sister. His parents, avid readers of parenting books,
weren't convinced that was such a good idea.

"What if he pinches her?" they discussed between themselves, reflecting upon current strategies for minimizing
sibling rivalry.

Even worse, they fretted, "What if he tries to smother her?"

But little Johnny was not to be deterred.

"We—her and me—have important business to discuss,"
he insisted.

Finally, while they waited within earshot outside the door,
Johnny's parents allowed him into the nursery by himself.

He gazed lovingly at his baby sister, leaned in over her
crib, and earnestly whispered, "Tell me about God. I'm starting to forget."

That four-year-old boy, still on the tightrope between his divine magnificence and the cultural training of Worldview 1.0, was grasping for his last breath of spiritual air, before being squeezed into the tight restrictions of the dominant cultural paradigm.

We Are Trained to Cut Off Large Parts of Ourselves

"I hate Spanx. They're so tight, who knows what you're cutting off?"
— JENNIFER COOLIDGE, AMERICAN ACTRESS

Anyone who has ever donned a pair of Spanx understands the reality of Worldview 1.0. We have squeezed our big, beautiful selves—our radiant, multidimensional spirits—into a tight, often-uncomfortable garment known as a body.

Like the four-year-old boy admitted to his baby sister, it didn't take long to pick up and adopt Worldview 1.0. It didn't take long to fall into lockstep with the beliefs and traditions of his culture, however false and limiting they may be.

As babies, we tune in to the adults around us. We see what they're drawn to. We notice how they behave, what they reject, and what they praise. We learn early on what is "beautiful" and what isn't. We learn how to think and feel about that god named money, damn him. We notice that the minute we get sick, we are trotted off to the doctor, learning quickly that we need something outside ourselves to heal.

When we are born, we are giant love generators. We radiate out a clear energy of light and incomparable joy. In a way, we're like dolphins, sending out our own special sonar of unconditional love. When this unconditional-love sonar runs up against the unhealed places in our culture, those places where distrust has developed or joy has been rejected, the sonar bounces back, giving us an unfamiliar reading, a "not love" reading. As our boundless joy hits these rigid beliefs and "thickened" emotions, we quickly learn to match our culture's energies, beliefs, and thoughts.

We learn to pinch off our gorgeous, clear love energy, allowing it to flow where we're trained it can flow, resigning ourselves to paralysis in other areas. Little by little, we learn the "correct" energetic-frequency rules, only allowing a small percentage of who we *really* are to radiate.

As babies, we love everything *so* much, especially our parents. If they inadvertently model a cutting off of large swaths of their power and energy, then . . . hey, we'll do it, too. We'll do whatever it takes to love. At our very core, pure, unadulterated love is what we are.

Lest you get the wrong idea, I'm not dissing anyone's parents. That neurosis went out with bell bottoms. Our parents did the best they could with the love sonar they sent out and the messages they received. They were once babies, too.

Cultural Paradigms Deprive You of Your Superpowers

*"When we drop our dreary stories . . . we are
provided for in every way."*
— ALBERTO VILLOLDO, CUBAN-BORN PSYCHOLOGIST AND SHAMAN

Before the age of five, pretty much everything we hear and experience is sucked up like a vacuum cleaner. Our brains, at that age, operate mainly in what scientists call theta waves. It's similar to REM sleep or hypnosis and works beautifully for picking up language, family nuances, and other things useful for making our way in the physical world. This mental, emotional, and physical framework is the programming that runs our lives. It's very useful when driving a car (imagine trying to relearn from scratch every time you get behind a steering

15

wheel) or brushing our teeth, but it wreaks havoc on our connection to the higher realms.

By relying on cataloged lessons from your family, your culture, and your past, you miss the teeming energy available in the atomic now. There is great substance within each present moment, just waiting to explode with goodness and magic and blessings. But by reapplying old, often inappropriate "cultural paradigms," you miss the magic—you completely overlook all the life-empowering data that's trying to stream to you from your inner, nonphysical self. This traps you in a web of defensive, limiting perceptions.

In fact, anytime we're not in the present moment, that tape loop kicks in and old constrictions and perceptual habits take over, infecting our thinking, our actions, and our beliefs. They're also a son of a bitch when attempting to be happy or manifest our dreams. None of these habits of thought are true, but because they stay buried for the most part, living in our subconscious like rats in the cellar, they subtly play out in our life experience anytime we're not "in the now." My friend Jay calls them BS—belief systems full of that other kind of BS. Unfortunately, these are the programs we use to explain, identify, and cope with our lives. They run most of the time even when we're affirming and intending other things.

If you have a smartphone and attempt to preserve its battery, you notice dozens of programs running at any one time, so many that your fingers get a regular workout swiping them away. All of these programs—or apps, as the case may be—have different frequencies, and all of them are fighting for battery power. Welcome to your consciousness. Still running BS from fifth grade, BS from the teacher who said, "Honey, you should stick to math. You have no artistic talent." Fighting for "battery power" with the BS of your mom saying, "Honey, there's no money for that right now."

This BS has taken over your consciousness, strangling your energy and, more often than not, running the show.

Meme a Little Meme for Me

"This spiritual truth is diametrically opposed to the values of our contemporary culture and the way it conditions people to behave."
— ECKHART TOLLE, AUTHOR OF THE POWER OF NOW

Our BS is such a valued part of our identities that it never occurs to us to question it. We regard these beliefs as gods, fearing them, trusting them, and completely acquiescing to them, without a single word of protest. These accepted beliefs are what British evolutionary biologist Richard Dawkins calls "memes." In short, the concept of memes explains how ideas, behaviors, and styles spread from person to person within a culture. Like viruses, they self-replicate, mutate, and entwine their mendacious tentacles throughout our lives.

Most of us are unaware of how big a role memes play in the way we experience life. They're like the kitchen junk drawer filled with a bunch of forgotten items: a dried-up magic marker, rusty scissors, old birthday cards from people we don't even remember, and keys that probably used to open something, although we're not sure what. For those of us interested in creating our own reality, it's important to clean out the junk drawer, to examine the memes that we and most everyone on planet Earth have come to regard as facts of life, as inalterable truths. Once we look behind the curtain, the BS is like the Great and not-so-Powerful Oz.

Here are 12 of the most popular memes from Worldview 1.0, memes that you might as well, as long as you're armed and actively fighting, take Beyoncé's advice and "put a ring" on them. Since you're already in a committed relationship with them anyway.

Each meme is followed by a Truth from Worldview 2.0, a Truth guaranteed to take the Mickey right out of your old beliefs.

1. MEME: The world is a menacing place. Our job is to put on our armor and work like hell to stay one step ahead of the terrorists, the supergerms, the dysfunctional stepmoms, and, of course, the zombies.

> WORLDVIEW **2.0:** *There is nothing to fear.*
> As *A Course in Miracles* repeatedly tells us,
> "We lay a heavy load upon ourselves with our
> insane beliefs that pain and sin [are] real. Pain is
> purposeless, without a cause and with no power
> to accomplish anything."

2. MEME: Life happens to me. "I'm an innocent bystander, a pitiful victim of circumstance, of weather, of disease, and, worse, of my own dysfunction. External events (those things from meme #1) constantly get in my face. The best I can do is learn to cope with these external events."

> WORLDVIEW **2.0:** *Life emanates from me.*
> "I create the world with my thoughts, my
> beliefs, and my energetic frequency."

3. MEME: Events happen; therefore, I feel bad. Most of our thoughts and feelings are programmed by the culture in which we are raised. We are trained at a very early age what makes us happy, which feelings go with which events, and how our moods should play out. We are trained to experience unhappy emotions, to blame these feeling on outside events, and to cry and moan about the unfairness of it all. We

18

are trained not to expect good things. In fact, all responsible people know that "shit happens."

I recently went through a death in my family. Death, as you know, has a pretty bad reputation. It was obvious to me that the little kids, the ones under 12, didn't view this passing the same as the adults. But after watching their parents, they quickly learned the appropriate script.

We are trained to worry about letting people down, being disliked, getting sick, being poor. We're trained to worry about pathogens, carcinogens, microwaves, plastic containers, preservatives, using mobile phones, and on and on.

> WORLDVIEW 2.0: *Without this training, joy is my natural state.* As Esther Hicks, author and inspirational speaker, once asked, "How come we only erect statues to war heroes? Where're the statues of surfer dudes?"

4. MEME: God is an entity outside of me. "Lowly 'little ole me' must appeal to His Majesty's benevolence, with fingers crossed that He'll somehow find time for me, a doubtful proposition, being as He's tied up fighting world hunger."

> WORLDVIEW 2.0: *God is a state of being, a loving energy that flows through me, sustains me, and surrounds me with light.* Although it's impossible to define or put into words, this "Radiant X," as poet Stephen Mitchell calls it, is the unnameable reality that causes everything to exist.

5. MEME: My job is to judge between right and wrong, black and white. And like comedian Gilda Radner used to say, "It's always something."

WORLDVIEW **2.0:** *My job is to create, not critique.* We have no ability to judge anything, and as soon as we do, we block the field of infinite potentiality that wants to come forth through us. Critiquing is not our job, people. While wearing these uncomfortable Spanx, we don't see the big picture. We use our subjective, limited viewfinder to play "ruler of the universe." It's as ridiculous as the blind man holding the tail of an elephant, thinking he now understands the monstrous beast.

Once we start "critiquing," we cease creating. By figuring things out, by labeling them, we restrict what we let into our awareness.

6. MEME: **I think, therefore I am.** Or in the words of Descartes: *Cogito, ergo sum.*

WORLDVIEW **2.0:** *What I think for the most part is irrelevant.* Say what? Isn't that the whole thesis of this book? Not exactly. Our thoughts are like harmless ants marching across a picnic blanket. They come, they go, they quickly flow right through . . . *until* we decide to gather them up, stare at them, and transform them into our reality. It is our attention to our thoughts that pull them into our reality. We decide which thoughts to feed, which thoughts to empower. Once we put energy into any thought, it begins accumulating mass, forming into "material" events and things.

7. MEME: **No pain, no gain.** The necessity of pain and suffering is such a living mythology and so entwined in our

culture that we blank it out like a refrigerator motor. In fact, if you believe Mel Gibson, whose movie *The Passion of the Christ* made horror movies look tame, it's even *holy* to be in pain.

We've become so accustomed to living in the "life sucks" paradigm that it never occurs to us that another reality, a happy reality, is possible. Pain, loneliness, and fear are the context within which we live our lives. We're so conditioned to wallow in misery that the concept of life as a joyous adventure seems impossible or even unnatural. Sure, we can buy that there will be happy events. In fact, we look forward to holidays and birthdays and time off work. But to believe that happiness is possible 24-7 is a big stretch.

The "life sucks" paradigm is really nothing but a bad habit, a rut we've been in since the first time our parents insisted we act our age. Looking for pain is nothing but a grossly irresponsible way of looking at the world.

> WORLDVIEW **2.0**: *There is no reason to struggle.* In fact, we don't actually have to "work" at anything. Once we let go—surrender to the universal flow of life—higher forces will take over and handle the details. Once we take sorrow off the throne, as *A Course in Miracles* describes our outlook in Worldview 1.0, enlightenment is our naturally occurring, organic state of being.

8. MEME: **It's important to look at my faults, to name my problems, and to strive to improve.** Aka: Wipe that silly grin off your face. Life is no laughing matter.

> WORLDVIEW **2.0**: *I already have everything I could ever want or need.* The only reason we see faults and problems is because we continue to look for faults and problems. Life, in the

new paradigm, is a game. And the fun is in the playing. Anytime we get tired of the roller coaster, we can head on over to the Lazy River.

9. MEME: **It's me and you (and I'm not so sure about you) against the world.** What in the heck are you thinking?

WORLDVIEW 2.0: *The universe has my back and is constantly sending me blessings, gifts, signs, and guidance.* And as for our brothers and sisters, see the letter of recommendation on page 24.

10. MEME: **I have to do everything myself.** Work, strive, keep on keeping on.

WORLDVIEW 2.0: *The only thing I have to do is follow my joy.* The universe will take care of everything else. Limitation and lack is a story we made up, no more real than the Easter Bunny.

Trying to force and manipulate reality is counterproductive in the new paradigm. Although the universal field is invisible (making it a lot harder to trust for some folks), it's actually far more tangible and powerful than forcing and grunting and groaning will ever be. By stepping back and connecting with the power of the universe, everything unfolds with ease and grace.

11. MEME: **I have to change. I'm scared to change. It's hard to change.** Help!

WORLDVIEW 2.0: *I can flip whatever I believe at any moment.* In fact, the flip side (say, lack versus abundance) is already there. The only reason you don't see it is you're tuned in to the frequency of lack.

It's important to remember that just because a reality exists now it's no more sturdy, infallible, or authoritative than any other reality. All physical realities are ephemeral and fluid. In Worldview 2.0, we understand that when we put our attention on one particular reality, it appears. And that when we simply withdraw our attention, it dissolves.

No one reality has authority over you. You, after all, are the creator.

12. MEME: I have to try really hard to be good enough. Aka: All men have sinned and fallen short of the glory of God.

WORLDVIEW **2.0:** *My worthiness is not at stake.* No 12 steps required. No obstacle courses, Spanx, or anything else getting in the way. Might as well sit back, relax, and enjoy the flight.

Letter of Recommendation for:

_____

[Fill in the blank for any Tom, Dick, or Harry on this planet. I don't care if the person is homeless, disabled, or wearing a black-and-white prison uniform.]

To whom it may concern:

_____ is a fabulous person. Given a little love, a little understanding, he/she will do remarkable things.

Sure, he/she has probably made a few mistakes, has probably done a few stupid things. But, boy, does he/she have a lot of love to give, a lot of ideas that can change the world.

By all means, take this person into your heart.

Hire him/her as your friend and confidant at your earliest possible convenience. Do not wait. Do not hesitate. There is nothing to be afraid of. This person is a treasure.

Sincerely yours,
Pam Grout

CHAPTER THREE

WELL, DUH!

"I'm sorry, man, but I've got magic.
I've got poetry in my fingertips."
— CHARLIE SHEEN, AMERICAN ACTOR

@Beastyboy90 to @PamGrout: I saw a butterfly in my
Thai boxing gym in the middle of winter. Can you
believe that?

@PamGrout: Definitely not surprised. As Phoebe
from *Friends* would say, "Well, duh!" Have a great
time with the rest of the experiments.

Okay, so this is the chapter where I gloat. Where I quote
Phoebe Buffay, who whenever someone complimented her—
whenever Ross or Monica or Chandler raved about her giving a good massage or writing a powerful song (well, come
to think of it, no one probably ever brought *that* up)—she'd
respond confidently with "Well, yeah?"

And that's what I want to say to all you readers who were
so dumbfounded that the experiments in *E-Squared* worked.

Lest you worry I will start singing "Smelly Cat," let me assure you that the only reason I can say "I *know!*" with sheer glee is because I now have reams of proof, file cabinets full of evidence that when you order something from the cosmic catalog of life, it's going to show up the minute you take down the barriers keeping it from your view. As soon as you release resistance and "get it" that the world always, without fail, has your back, the party can begin.

But before we throw out the confetti, I have to ask. And this is an important question you should also ask yourself.

Why are you surprised?

There's something a whole lot greater manning the dials here on this crazy planet than you, me, or even Jimmy Fallon. And as I hope the *E-Squared* experiments proved, this "whole lot greater" is infinitely more fun than anything we can touch or see with our retinas. We're all connected to this monster universal energy flow, and good stuff is supposed to be rushing toward us. That's what's natural.

The *only* reason you're not aware of this nonstop stream of blessings and miracles is because you're looking the other way. Worldview 1.0 might suggest you're an impartial spectator looking at an objective reality.

But Worldview 2.0 is very clear. We are not helpless victims waiting for the other shoe to drop.

The world we see emanates from us. We cannot even look at anything without affecting it. We're in a constant two-step with the energy force, but when *moi* and *vous* and our crazy guilt complexes and insecurities sit on the sidelines, holding up scorecards like we're some *Dancing with the Stars* judges, we hang heavy opaque curtains between us and the Big Universal Flow.

People, it's time to say, "Well, duh!" It's time to use our thoughts and consciousness to leverage magic.

Throwing Out Confetti

*"Focus is the most magical tool we have. It's the most
powerful aspect of our minds. It's the letter in the
universal mailbox, the genie in the lamp."*
— MARIAN LANSKY, AMERICAN GRAPHIC ARTIST

On New Year's Eve 2012, I took a big stick and on the
beach at Tybee Island, Georgia, wrote this proclamation in
the sand: *"E-Squared* will become an international bestseller."
And then I let the ocean and its waves take it out into the
world.

Admittedly, it's a rather unconventional marketing strategy. A billboard at least would have been lit at night. But last
I checked, it seems to be working.

E-Squared has been translated into 30-some languages. It
sat squarely on the *New York Times* bestseller list for 20 weeks,
several weeks at number one. And I hear from people all over
the world, sometimes in languages I can't begin to translate.
All of them seem to Love. This. Book.

Every day, I get e-mails and Facebook messages from
excited readers with some variation of this theme: "Holy s--t!
This stuff really works."

The spiritual principles I outlined in *E-Squared* are nothing new. We've heard about these concepts for hundreds of
years, but until this book, they'd never been broken down
into bite-size pieces. They'd never been scientifically tested.

I knew these nine principles worked in my own life. I've
used them quite successfully to jet around the world, to stay
in five-star hotels, to meet fascinating people, and, when
needed, to manifest money. What I didn't know is just how
well they'd translate into other people's experience. As I've
told interviewers, there is no way, after hearing all the stories,

that I could ever doubt these principles again. If anything, my certainty in their merit has grown to Sequoia proportions.

I could barely keep up with all the stories that landed like jumbo jets of joy in my in-box every morning. I received updates from this new cast of friends about everything from blossoming new relationships to unexpected money sailing in. My all-time favorites were from readers just beginning to trust in the beneficence of the universe, those finally getting it that limitation and lack is just a crazy story we made up. As one reader told me, "The part of me that is so septic has suffered a big blow."

These *oh-wow!* tales were so much fun that I spent most of 2013 with a perpetual smile on my face, pumping my fist into the air so often that my right bicep began to resemble Dwayne (the Rock) Johnson's. Guess I'll have to begin pumping with my left arm when this book comes out.

I've gotten pictures, tales of "coincidences," and incontrovertible evidence that the universe is just waiting for us to catch up, just waiting for us to begin using this energy that has always been available for our enjoyment and well-being. The butterfly stories alone could fill the Library of Congress.

Butterflies, in case you're new to the party, are one of the "signs" I suggested people look for to prove *E-Squared*'s Volkswagen Jetta Principle, which states: "You impact the field and draw from it according to your beliefs and expectations."

People spotted butterflies on pie in the middle of the desert, on toilet paper, on lapels in doctors' offices, and on casino slot machines, to name just a few that spring to mind. Some people even wrote to ask, "How do I turn the butterflies off?"

Once you start looking for something, it seems to multiply as fast as Mickey Mouse's broom in the *Sorcerer's Apprentice.* One reader who decided to look for clowns reported that he now sees clowns everywhere: on posters in the London Tube, in ads in inflight magazines, on buses, on vans, on videos (most recent example was a film where Denzel Washington and Mark Wahlberg robbed a bank wearing clown masks), and that every time he and his wife get in the car, they hear the track "Clown" by Emeli Sandé.

Not surprisingly, in a world focused on material things, I got reams of stories about manifesting unexpected money. Readers found $5 here or a lucky penny there or received notice of a decrease in, say, their insurance premiums. The record so far is . . . hope you're sitting down . . . $100,000 in five days. People were sent flowers, led to signs (actual signs) that said things like, "If you're waiting for a sign, this is it." One reader decided to manifest purple and was invited to a women's roller derby in an arena with thousands of purple seats.

So I guess it's fair to say that *E-Squared* has become a phenomenon. It has gone from being a funny title on a little black book to a verb. Instead of "making intentions," people say they're E-Squaring their desires. As in, "I want a ticket to the Super Bowl. I'll just E-Square it." Or, "I need to know today whether or not to have that operation. Guess I better E-Square it."

Several friends suggested I write a book with all the remarkable stories, a sort of *Chicken Soup for the Manifester's Soul*. Since I'm rather partial to writing my own stories (and also because my old laptop crashed when I was in Namibia, dashing the file of stories I was earnestly keeping), I decided I'd honor their request by concluding this chapter with a few of my favorites. Some of these stories are direct quotations. Some are retold in my words. All of them are fascinating reminders that we live in a participatory universe. God, to use a term most of us are familiar with, created a world that continues to create itself.

If nothing else, recapping a few stories is a clever ploy for tricking you into reviewing the key principles from *E-Squared*.

E-Squared *Redux and a Few Campfire Tales*

"You gain strength, courage and confidence by every experience in which you really stop to look fear in the face. You must do the thing which you think you cannot do."
— ELEANOR ROOSEVELT, FORMER FIRST LADY

The nine energy principles I wrote about in *E-Squared* are still the bedrock, the foundation for learning to master your own reality. And even though I like to think they stand on their own two feet, it never hurts to hear this kind of message again, especially since the old-school conditioning is so ingrained and painfully easy to fall back on. When learning to override outdated cultural paradigms, it's important to practice the new paradigm over and over again until it becomes second nature. Until you don't have to think about it. Until noticing miracles is just how you roll.

1. The Dude Abides Principle:
There Is an Invisible Energy Force or
Field of Infinite Possibilities

"There is an invisible plane supporting the visible one."
— JOSEPH CAMPBELL, AMERICAN MYTHOLOGIST

In this experiment, which doubles as an ultimatum, I asked people to give the field exactly 48 hours to make its presence known, to demand a clear, unmistakable sign that could not be written off as coincidence. Here's a sample of some of the blessings:

- "I found $20,000 in Apple stock I did not know I had. And a producer from England called about doing a dating reality show in the U.K."

- "I didn't want to wait for 48 hours. So instead I set the deadline for my airplane flight today. And guess what? I sat next to a famous person on the plane. The guitar player from Lynyrd Skynyrd."

- "I read your first experiment to my hubby, had him make the request of an unexpected gift, and that night, totally unexpected, he won a $1,500 Smart TV."

- "For the first experiment, I asked the universe for a sign that I 100 percent could not dispute. The next morning, I went to my desk to get some work done and turned on the radio. Guess what song was playing? 'Johanna' by Kool and the Gang! It's been *years* since I heard that song. Since my name is Johanna, as they crooned, 'Johanna, I love you,' I knew the universe was telling me I was loved!"

- "I was raised an only child and *always* wished for brothers and sisters. For years, I thought I had no other living adult relatives besides two distant cousins in Southern California. I gave the Dude 48 hours on a Thursday at 10:00 P.M. One of my cousins left me a message the next morning . . . and by Monday, I was friends with more than 40 family members, mostly cousins and second cousins, whom I had just moments before not known existed."

- "I went to a plein air event to paint. I sold both paintings and then sold 15 more at the Sunday show. Two years ago, I went to this show and sold *nothing!*"

- "Out of the blue an acquaintance who knew I was engaged insisted on gifting me a $7,000 wedding dress. I'm a single mother of four—most of my cars were worth less than that until a couple of years ago. Then, thanks to a constellation of curious circumstances, I got to spend an afternoon shopping, lunching, and meditating with another one of my favorite authors, Lissa Rankin."

- "I manifested $10,000 from a Catholic priest I hadn't heard from in four years, and I'm not even Catholic anymore. I'm not kidding, a $10,000 gift with no strings attached."

2. The Volkswagen Jetta Principle: You Impact the Field and Draw from It According to Your Beliefs and Expectations

"There is nothing more deceptive than an obvious fact."
— Arthur Conan Doyle, British author

To prove this principle, I gave people 48 hours to pull from the field some simple thing like sunset-beige cars, butterflies, or feathers. Here's what happened:

- "If this wasn't so insanely awesome and completely out of my realm of expectation, I wouldn't bother sharing. I stayed home all day working on my laptop, so I was pretty sure I wouldn't see any green cars or yellow butterflies. The experiment was on my mind, because I knew I still had tomorrow. After dinner, my boyfriend (who had no knowledge of my experiment) asked me to come into the living room because he had something to show me. As an early birthday present, he made this for me . . . it's a butterfly house. There are butterflies in it! In my house! I get to look at them for a few days, and then we set them free. I literally couldn't speak for ten minutes. I'm hoping the green cars stay on the road tomorrow."

- "I wanted to be sure, so I asked the universe to show me different car colors . . . from purple to yellow to orange. And yes, I saw them all. However, I'm stubborn and wanted to be sure that the universe was listening and that it was not just a coincidence . . . the car colors I saw were different but by no means unrealistic. I decided to come up with the most obscure combination of colors I could think of . . . a pink truck with white polka dots. Two days later I drove by a pink truck with white polka dots!"

- "I was in the second half of Experiment #2 and was actively looking for purple feathers—in the middle of winter in Colorado. I was skeptical. My cousin lost his son in the floods in Boulder last September, and I often follow updates from his friends and family on his Facebook page. Guess what Wesley was wearing in one of the pictures I had yet to see? A headband with a purple feather tucked in it. *Blown away, truly, blown away!"

For those who still believe in and are frustrated by the concept of time (I know, it's a pretty convincing illusion), this one's for you:

- "I focused on manifesting a red rubber bouncy ball (another zinger, I thought). Forty-eight hours later . . . no ball . . . that was three weeks ago. I wrote it off as not being focused enough. Fast-forward . . . no sh*t, today, at the same intersection where I saw the burnt-orange car, a red rubber bouncy ball literally rolled across the street with the wind, right across my path . . . as if taunting me. I jumped out, dodged cars, and picked it up. Holding it now."

3. The Alby Einstein Principle: You, Too, Are a Field of Energy

"I couldn't even make this stuff up."
— Drew, reader of *E-Squared*

Experiment #3, which proves we humans are actually moving currents of energy, was a real hoot. In it, I explained how to turn metal coat hangers into what I call "Einstein wands." Using these homemade energy wands, people could watch their thoughts in action. Positive, happy thoughts "opened" the wands. Negative thoughts caused them to turn in on each other.

Leslie Draper, an intuitive from Oklahoma who calls herself the Bible Belt Mystic, went to her local dry cleaner and got 50 hangers to fashion into wands for all her clients, including several medical doctors, who were, as she described it, "blown away." She even made a fabulous YouTube video of the wands, one of dozens out there on the Internet, visibly demonstrating how our thoughts interact with the universe.

One reader from Florida told me he took them to his local bar to impress his buddies. Another suggested I manufacture them to sell at Toys "R" Us. And I also discovered that metal coat hangers are no longer easy to find (maybe they never were?) in Scandinavian countries.

4. The Abracadabra Principle: Whatever You Focus on Expands

"By believing passionately in something that does not yet exist, we create it."
— NIKOS KAZANTZAKIS, GREEK WRITER AND PHILOSOPHER

In this experiment, I asked people to put in an order from the Cosmic Catalog of Life. To make an intention to draw something into their lives, something simple, something that wouldn't immediately bring up major resistance. Here are a few stories readers shared:

- "This is so amazing! I sent myself a postcard, like you did. I wrote, as if someone else, that they loved what they saw at my photography exhibition and would call to offer me a contract. Well, I sent it on Thursday, and by Friday I was offered two contracts. I hadn't even received the postcard yet. I am now a true believer. It's just up to me to decide what I want."

- "I requested 'free money.' Not much happened for a few days . . . then—*boom*—*three* random clients sent me gift cards (a total of $160 at Starbucks and $50 at Target), and I went to a party and was asked to tell a few jokes to the crowd at dinner. They sent me a check for $250 . . . I'm up to $460 in a week."

- "Today I went for a walk, and halfway in I wished I had brought money with me so I could get a coffee. I had no money, so I tried an experiment. I put it out that I would find some money on the ground, enough for a coffee. I thought, *There has to be a way for me to have a coffee without any money.* I scoured the ground as I continued on. Then I came to a park; I looked up, and right in front of me was a sign that said FREE COFFEE AND CUP-CAKES and a van with a guy who made me a latte!"

- "I am manifesting all over the place and have just pulled off a whopper! I had never heard of Lawrence Block before reading *E-Squared,* but your mention of his book *Write for Your Life* gave me instant goose bumps, and I decided I had to have a copy. All inquiries in Australia led to dead ends: out of print and definitely unavailable. I logged on to his website—prolific, ain't he?—and e-mailed asking if perhaps he had a spare copy under his pillow. The reply, from David Trevor, was that there might be some copies somewhere. He would check and, if found, would list them on eBay and would notify me of same. I awoke next day to his e-mail and a link to eBay, where the remaining stash of 25 just-found copies (auto-graphed by Larry Block) were now listed for sale. Excitedly I attempted to purchase, but alas, the last one vanished as I processed my payment. I e-mailed David again, expressing my devastation. His empathetic reply was that if I didn't mind a 'secondhand' copy of the book, he had one left that he would be happy to sell me (having been the catalyst for the eBay frenzy). *The copy that had belonged to LB's* (now-deceased) *mother.* It had recently been returned to them, and *it's auto-graphed by LB to his mum! How cool is that!* I am so thrilled! Can't wait to read it."

- "I asked for some free meat. Tonight when my friend came over to drop her girl off for the weekend she brought two meat lover's pizzas and two packs of chicken chips."

- "I said, 'I am ready for a Billy Joel concert,' even though this past summer he announced no more concerts. Well, two days later, he's playing New Year's Eve at the Barclay Center. I think I'm on to something big."

- "Friday night I decided to demand the earring I had lost. That might not seem so important to the average person, but these earrings were a gift from my son, Dustin. He fell from a cliff in 2009 at the age of 17 and was truly our golden boy. I was devastated. One day last summer I looked in the mirror—to see one of the earrings gone, and I was frantic. Today the bathroom drain was partially clogged, so my husband lifted up the plunger a little to allow the water to drain better. When I went in to brush my teeth, I saw all the hair entwined on the bottom of the plunger, so I got a toothpick to pull it out. That is when I saw something round, and using the toothpick, I pulled out my earring. In less than 48 hours after giving my ultimatum, I got my earring back. I'm a happy girl!"

5. The Dear Abby Principle:
Your Connection to the Field Provides Accurate and Unlimited Guidance

"We either make ourselves miserable, or we make ourselves happy. The amount of work is the same."
— CARLOS CASTANEDA, PERUVIAN-AMERICAN ANTHROPOLOGIST

This experiment encouraged people to give up their belief in separation and to open to the possibility that answers to any question are available 24-7.

- "I lost my diamond necklace that I have worn almost every day for 33 years a little over a month ago. We were smoking some meat yesterday on our grill. I was gone for a couple of hours walking our dogs and came back to check on the meat, and there on the ground in front of me was the diamond necklace that had been gone for a month. It looked like someone had just cleaned it in jewelry cleaner. Did it go to another dimension and then make its way back?"

- "I had asked the FP a couple of days prior, that if I was pregnant, to show me two visibly pregnant women before I got on the plane for my connecting flight to NYC. As I exited the first plane to catch my connection, I walked right by the first one. Our plane was delayed an hour, so I went to the bookstore, was looking at magazines, and one of them literally flew off the shelf and landed open on the ground. With guess what? A picture of a *very* pregnant Jennifer Love Hewitt.

- "I asked God/the universe which of three books I should focus on and write first. I listed the three I have been working on—a novel, a nonfiction book, and my life story. About halfway through the 48 hours, I saw a Facebook post from someone who *never* posts quotations that said, 'When writing the story of your life, don't let anyone else hold the pen.' Wow! That's all I can say! Wow!"

- "I asked for something to bring a big smile to my face. I was texting as I entered the building for Mastin Kipp's Daily Love workshop, not paying much attention, and looked up as I held the door open for someone—and it was Mastin Kipp himself. Big smile!"

- "I lost a gold ring while gardening over three years ago, so after reading this book, I asked the FP to find it for me as an experiment. About a week later I was cleaning under the stove and found the ring—I was really amazed! How did it get there? That, to me, really demonstrated the principle, more than if I had found it in the garden. This stuff works!"

- "My question was, *Should I go ahead with my planned home refinance?* I live in a rural part of Missouri with train tracks in front of my home. As a train sped past my house, I was looking at the graffiti. In bold, large letters was the word NOPE. Go figure, right? This morning, I was sitting outdoors and I said aloud, 'Am I safe to assume that "nope" was my neon-sign message?' At that instant, I hear the *ding-ding-ding* of the railroad crossing, and here comes another train. The train was heavy with coal, requiring two engines to pull it. Both doors on the second engine were wide-open and swinging in the wind. This is unheard of. The very next car was labeled with this graffiti: FEEL FREE TO ASK US. I LOVE YOU. I LOVE YOU."

6. The Superman Principle:
Your Thoughts and Consciousness Impact Matter

*"The lesson begins with three words. If you never
remember anything else I have told you, remember
these words like a mantra: Thoughts precede everything.
Thoughts. Precede. Everything."*

— PAT HELDMAN, AMERICAN AUTHOR

This experiment, which involved growing green-bean
seeds in an egg carton, was popular with moms and their
kids. Duplicating an experiment done by Dr. Gary Schwartz
at the University of Arizona, I asked readers to send light,
love, and intention to one row of seeds and basically ignore
the other. I have a whole gallery of photos showing that the
seeds that were lovingly regarded sprouted and grew faster
and taller than their ignored counterparts.

And I'll also share this e-mail:

- "Just a quick note of fun and frolic . . . I couldn't
  bear to just toss my sprouted beans after the experiment a few months back, so I found the most
  fertile place I could find in our pretty barren apart-
  ment building and transplanted them. This morning, lo and behold . . . I have fresh green beans!
  This coming from a 'brown thumb' in previous at-
  tempts to get anything to grow or blossom."

7. The Jenny Craig Principle:
Your Thoughts and Consciousness Provide the
Scaffolding for Your Physical Body

*"There are no physical laws in the universe.
They're more like suggestions."*

— SRI AUROBINDO, INDIAN SAINT

This experiment proved that our thoughts are in a continuous dance with our bodies and with our food. In the last hour I've been working on this chapter, I've received two e-mails from readers who say they've lost major poundage from doing the Jenny Craig experiment. That means doing nothing but blessing your food and throwing away old patterns of chastising yourself before eating.

The following are sample results in pounds lost by doing nothing but changing thoughts:

- 3

- 5

- 2

- 2½

Another reader lost 18 pounds by doing one thing: "I gave up guilt. I let myself eat anything I wanted."

8. The 101 Dalmatians Principle: You Are Connected to Everyone and Everything Else in the Universe

"Those who don't believe in magic will never find it."
— ROALD DAHL, AUTHOR OF CHARLIE AND THE CHOCOLATE FACTORY

Also known as nonlocality, this experiment asked readers to send messages to people without the use of e-mail, letters, or loud explosions.

- "I just started Experiment #8 today (11/19/13) at 8:30 A.M. I decided to ask for two people to call me, a lifelong friend I've known for almost 40 years and an old girlfriend. I haven't spoken with either of them for quite a while. I made my intention. I even opened the front door and said each of their full names and added, 'Call me.' Within 15 minutes I got a call from the old girlfriend."

- "I was missing an old friend who hasn't called in two years. I sent the intention to the FP, and she called within 30 minutes."

- "I recently read your book and read about the nail incident. I am wrestling with this whole manifesting concept, and I was fascinated and, yes, envious about it. I said to the universe, 'Boy, I wish I had a mind-blowing experience like that nail one.' And not expecting to have one, I moved on. When I went to get dressed this morning, I was standing in my closet and looked down at something on the floor. It was a nail! I howled. Yes, the field does have a sense of humor. I could almost hear it say, 'You wanted a nail?' If I hadn't read your book, I may have found that nail and would have thought no more about it except to wonder what the heck it was doing there. So for me this truly has been an illumination of how we are connected . . . crazy."

- "The most recent experiment I did was mind-blowing! It's the one that instructed 'send a message to someone you know using the concept of nonlocality.' You suggested focusing on someone I'd already met, and you also mentioned Bruce Rosenblum's claim that once a person has met another and shaken his/her hand, 'you are forever entangled.' This grabbed my attention, because the person I wanted to focus on was my great-great-aunt Neva, whom I have never met—she died, single and childless, before I was born. I inherited a ring that had belonged to her, and since we have both worn this ring, I figured it would count as a 'handshake.' And since we are related by blood, I also figured that could count as our having 'met.' My great-great-aunt's untimely death left a big gaping hole in my genealogy chart, because she had always been a family mystery, and no one knew for sure when or where she'd died. So, I tried your experiment while commuting to work the other morning. I spoke my thoughts like this: *Hi there, Neva, it's your great-grandniece here. I want to know what happened to you, where you died, and when, so your story can be passed down to my kids and their descendants. Will you please help me out here? Thanks!* During my lunch break, I was surfing around on the Web when I got an Ancestry.com alert that I had a new genealogy fact. What is so weird is that the death record was in California, where I had searched before—several times—without success. Suddenly the record was right there: Los Angeles County, California, September 3, 1926. But how did I get the record at all—that very afternoon? How did the record just appear the very day I 'talked' to Neva and asked for her help? . . . This is amazing! Your experiment even works for people who have been dead for well over 80 years!"

9. The Fish and Loaves Principle: The Universe Is Limitless, Abundant, and Strangely Accommodating

"Let us cease walking through life blinded by darkness and confusion, seeing shadows on every wall and corner."
— MICHELE LONGO O'DONNELL, AMERICAN AUTHOR

To prove this principle, I asked readers to spend 48 hours tracking goodness and beauty. I got the idea from paleontologist Stephen Jay Gould, who called it our duty, our holy responsibility, to record and honor the victorious weight of all the innumerable little kindnesses that he said were all too often unnoted and invisible.

Because these lists were unwieldy (literally hundreds of thousands of good things happen every day), and impossible to publish, I decided to devote this section to a few of the hundreds of humorous stories that came in. The FP definitely appreciates a good joke.

- "I was running late for a friend's birthday dinner, desperately looking for a parking place. After many drives around the car park, I decided to 'E-Square' it. I flippantly said to my kids, 'What we need is a movie to finish and then everyone will start leaving.' With that command, a parking space opened right up outside the restaurant. About the same time, a fire truck pulled up right outside the cinema and hundreds of people flooded out. Not only did one movie finish (just as requested), but also a fire prompted the theater to close down and evacuate all 12 theaters."

- "I got my 'little gift' hand delivered by a Jehovah's Witness this morning at 10. At exactly 21 hours after I started the experiment, a booklet was delivered that stated on the back, 'God is a type of infinite spirit.' He also has a great sense of humor."

- "This morning, while at breakfast at a local restaurant, I asked the universe for an unexpected gift within the next 48 hours. After running errands, I arrived home to find my gift: six baby ducklings paddling around in my swimming pool. My husband was dumbfounded. I have no idea where they came from. Not only is the universe fast, but it also has a sense of humor! What a delightful gift. My children and I rounded up the ducklings and walked over to the pond of a nearby golf course."

- "One of the most synchronous things I've ever witnessed happened to me when I started reading this book. My wife was filling out some online forms from her phone, as she does each evening. Sometimes the 'captchas' that she has to fill out to prove she is human are a little odd or quite witty, so she reads them out loud. The other night she got 'The Dude Abides,' which she thought was odd, and I kinda thought, *Huh, interesting phrase,* and thought no more about it. Thirty minutes later I started reading *E-Squared,* and the first experiment is, of course, 'The Dude Abides.' The fact that the experiment is to ask for undeniable proof of the existence of 'God' that can't be explained by coincidence just blew us away."

PART II

THE EXPERIMENTS

"So I'm curious, my fellow creators. Since you and I are in charge of making a New Earth—not just breaking down the dying culture—where do we begin? What stories do we want at the heart of our experiments? What questions will be our oracles?

"Here's what I say: In the New Earth we're creating, we will ridicule the cult of doom and gloom, and embrace the cause of zoom and boom. We will laugh at the stupidity of evil and hate; we will summon the brilliance to praise and create. No matter how upside down it all may appear, we will have no fear, because we know this big secret: All of creation is conspiring to shower us with blessings. Life is crazily in love with us—brazenly and innocently in love with us."

— ROB BREZSNY, FROM *PRONOIA IS THE ANTIDOTE FOR PARANOIA*

THE PRELIMINARIES

Important Guidelines for Unlocking the Magic

"Theories might inspire you,
but experiments will advance you."
— AMIT KALANTRI, INDIAN AUTHOR

cor·ol·lar·y
ˈkôrəˌlerē, ˈkärə-

1. forming a proposition that follows from one already proved.

2. a direct or natural consequence or result.

As you know if you've read *E-Squared*, I believe that spirituality and abstruse concepts such as thought creates matter should be proven, not taken on faith. For years, these principles have made for stimulating dinner conversation, interesting sermon fodder.

But because we've only been theorizing about them, not putting them into practice, our world has not been rocked in the radical way it needs to be. Without practical application, these principles are little but abstractions and feel-good woo-woo! This book, like its predecessor, emphasizes application and experience, not theology.

The fact that you are connected to everyone and everything in the universe is not just mind-blowing news. It's something you should be using. The fact that your thoughts are energy waves being broadcast out into this giant field of infinite potentiality is something you should be aware of and deploying on a moment-by-moment basis. Some might even suggest we've squandered 100 years merely poking at these principles, discussing them at the watercooler rather than actively using them to make our world, our lives, and our relationships better.

Each of the following chapters presents a corollary to the spiritual principles from *E-Squared* and an empirical science experiment to demonstrate its validity. All of them are designed to prove that you are connected to the field of infinite potentiality, to demonstrate that quantum physics isn't just a compelling philosophy but a useful tool.

The Real World Is Better Than Any Lab

"Be forewarned, applying these teachings may be damaging to your beliefs, disorienting to your mind, and distressing to your ego."
— ADYASHANTI, AMERICAN SPIRITUAL TEACHER

Guglielmo Marconi, the Italian inventor who pioneered long-distance radio transmission, won the Nobel Prize in 1909 for sending vibratory radio waves 2,000 miles across the Atlantic Ocean.

But when he first suggested that frequencies of energy could be transmitted without wires, people thought he was nuts. When he wrote to the Italian Ministry of Posts and

Telegraphs explaining the idea of wireless telegraphy, he was referred to an insane asylum.

"Everyone knows that's impossible," he was told by detractors, who scoffed at the crazy experiments he conducted in his parents' attic.

So, yes, believing that our thoughts, dreams, and beliefs are being transmitted out into the universe and shaping our destiny is not for everyone. But it's certainly better than habitually focusing on what's *not* working, better than concentrating on what *can't* happen.

Remember that as long as your consciousness refuses to embrace a potential new possibility, it remains beyond your purview. Who'd have thought 150 years ago that you could walk into a room, flip a switch, and get light? Or bend metal into a machine that could fly over the ocean?

Feel free to conduct the experiments in chronological order, jump around, or do all nine in one day. It's really up to you. Create your own rules. The important thing is to play and have fun.

I've found it helpful to write my experiments down, to document my thoughts and feelings before I start and then again after. Because we tend to "forget" or edit out experiences that don't jibe with our preconceived cultural scripts, getting it in writing helps build confidence. Just like we forget our dreams if we don't write them down upon waking, we tend to forget "nontraditional" experiences if we don't record them. I love going back over my notebooks and realizing how many amazing manifestations I promptly threw out the window of my waking consciousness. I've included lab report sheets for just that purpose.

I'd also like to suggest that you keep these three phrases in the back of your mind.

1. It's easy.

2. It doesn't matter.*

3. Anyone can do this.

Please Do *Disturb*
(or *Why You Should Always Play with Your Toys*)

> *"I think that in the discussion of natural problems
> we ought to begin not with the Scriptures, but with
> experiments, and demonstrations."*
> — GALILEO GALILEI, ITALIAN ASTRONOMER

The fact that the universe is responsive to our thoughts is vital information. The fact that you can't observe anything without affecting it is of paramount importance. But when I say *paramount,* I don't mean it should be buttoned down and clamped to structure. In fact, the more fun you have with these experiments, the better they work.

In the current worldview, play and experimentation are often preempted by the need to get serious, to eliminate mistakes. Worldview 1.0 also suggests that *important* things like God and science and energy are not to be played with. They're concepts reserved for experts. Those of us without credentials? Keep out!

But that's ridiculous. If I'm connected to everyone (and according to quantum mechanics, I am), then why shouldn't *I* be advancing civilization along with Stephen Hawking? If my glance is able to convey love, why shouldn't I be pursuing that superpower at every opportunity?

So here's what I propose.

---

* These experiments don't matter because in the end, life always turns out okay. They should be approached in a lighthearted, fun way. When we think things MATTER SO MUCH, when we make them heavy and ponderous, we block the results.

Let's turn these world-changing experiments into a party for all. Let's get everybody on board. Let's make it so much fun that nobody will be able to resist.

The experiments in this book, corollaries to the experiments in *E-Squared,* are democratic, easy for anyone to try, and set up in the same scientific method used by real scientists in real labs. But to undertake these as serious endeavors where mistakes aren't tolerated or where fun is not allowed is the wrong attitude. That hoity-toity, let's-eliminate-any-possibility-of-error MO only subverts the results and keeps us stuck in the twisted world where defenses reign. I believe everyone should get into the sandbox and make a mess.

My philosophy? Make. It. Fun.

Albert Einstein himself said that fun and brilliant new discoveries go hand in hand. He posited that great minds ignored rule books, valued creativity, and were not bound by structure. The standardized tests and seven rules for this or eight steps to that are veritable guarantors of mediocrity. Einstein's creativity was, in his own words, "playful, muscular and visual."

In fact, the more fun you make this, the quicker it will work for you. Being in a playful state releases you from the left-brain trap. It allows you to let go of the mental constructs of limited space and time.

We Don't Need More Beliefs— We Need More Practice

"In everyone's life, at some time, our inner fire goes out. It is then burst into flame by an encounter with another human being."
— ALBERT SCHWEITZER, GERMAN-FRENCH MISSIONARY PHYSICIAN AND HUMANITARIAN

I'd like to mention one last strategy. Get a group together. There is nothing like compadres on the path of enlightenment to encourage, celebrate, and challenge your personal perceptions. When I say *group,* it doesn't have to be huge. Two, as far as I'm concerned, can be a group.

Neuroscientists have discovered that humans reverberate to the actions and emotions of the people around them. This unspoken but ongoing communication is why someone yawning can make you yawn even if you slept ten hours the night before. It's why bouncing around in Zumba with a group or applauding with a concert audience makes us feel so happy.

This resonance is why I'm part of two power posses here in my hometown of Lawrence, Kansas. We get together weekly (one is twice a month) to talk about quantum physics, spirituality, and the idea that consciousness creates the foundation of our lives. I walk out of those groups—no, I should say I *dance* out of those groups—buzzing with joy and love and creative ideas. Which creates even more joy and love . . . and makes me wonder, *Why doesn't everyone do this?*

So if you're not in a group, get in one. Enlist friends to join you in goofing around with these principles. I use the phrase *goofing around* on purpose. It's vital not to take any of this too seriously. Again, the more you can laugh, the more you can turn it into a game, the better these experiments work.

The Vital Portal to the FP

"In an exuberant state of joy, you are at peace with everything about you . . . there is no thing unconquerable, no thing unreachable."
— RAMTHA, SPIRIT ENTITY CHANNELED BY J. Z. KNIGHT

A couple of years ago, a member of one of my power posses made a New Year's resolution to "never say no to fun." That meant if anyone asked her to go to a concert or go out dancing or out to lunch, she was committed to say, "You betcha!"

She had begun to notice that she was turning down invitations because, well, she's a mom and she had a busy day or she was tired or . . . you get the idea. There are a million rational reasons adults can give for declining an offer to enjoy themselves. Kids, she noted, never turned down fun. They were constantly in search of the next good time. Teenagers, too, would never spurn a party, no matter how late or how much they were going to piss off their parents by sneaking out the bedroom window.

When was the tipping point? At what point did we begin rejecting the chance for joy and glee?

What she discovered during her year of "just saying yes" is that the energy she thought she was going to conserve by staying home actually grew. The tired feeling that had previously compelled her to give the other answer completely disappeared.

And now, she says, "I don't even have to think about it. I always say yes to fun."

Power Posse Rules
(Which, of Course, You Are Free to Shred)

- **Commit to discussing only what's going right.** There are 9,387,642,428,000 groups discussing what is wrong, working to right injustice. But in these groups, be honest, be real, but focus on the blessings and miracles coming into your life.

- **Commit to having fun.**

- **Commit to being overjoyed.**

That's it. Go forth and prosper.

Raining Cats and Blogs

In the launch of *E-Squared,* Hay House sent me a book called *Platform* by Michael Hyatt. Basically, it's a primer for becoming a social-media maven. They FedExed it to me, insisted it was required reading. Since marketing was never my forte, I figured what the heck. Usually, I'm too busy writing the next travel article or the next profile for *People* magazine to get involved in the logistics of marketing my books. But since my 15 previous books didn't exactly reach astounding pinnacles of glory, I decided to give it a try, to devote some time to social-media marketing.

The main theme is to start blogging and do it daily. This didn't particularly appeal to me. I'm a professional writer, after all, and I write for pay. But I figured it was a way to conduct my own experiment with an oft-repeated principle of *A Course in Miracles* that states: "To give and receive are one in Truth."

I remember very clearly that first post I put up. I was quaking in my boots to put myself out there like that. Of course, at the time, I had all of five followers. (Thanks, Mom!) But as I began writing these blog posts, cementing in the powerful ideas I proposed in *E-Squared,* I came to realize that (a) I love these principles, (b) I love blogging, and (c) I love all the positive feedback. I lapped it up like a kitten laps up warm milk.

So throughout Part II, I'm including a post straight from my blog that illustrates each experiment, starting with these preliminaries. Hope you enjoy!

Lions and Gladiators and Problems, Oh My!

"Everything you have taught yourself has made your power more and more obscure to you."
— A COURSE IN MIRACLES

I'm not psychic, but I'm pretty sure that 100 years from now (hopefully sooner), future generations are going to look back on our belief in separation and limits and wonder, *What were they thinking? How could they be so misinformed?*

They'll scratch their heads at our refusal to use our innate power in much the same way we look back upon the Roman circuses. *Are you kidding me?* we think. *How could thousands of people sit around drinking wine and being entertained by lions ripping gladiators apart?*

They'll consider it a pitiable curiosity that we treated ourselves this way, that we chose to suffer when right on the other side of the veil is everything we could possibly want.

My lesson in *A Course in Miracles* today is "Let me recognize my problems have been solved." In a nutshell, it encourages you, me, and everyone else who is following along with the *Course* to free ourselves of problems that do not exist.

A Course in Miracles advocates the idea that consciousness creates the material world. It says we humans decide in advance how we're going to experience life, that we choose beforehand what we want to see.

We weaken ourselves when we put all our energy into trying to solve our problems. By focusing on a mindless process (identifying problems, studying them, following blogs about them), instead of putting our attention on what we *really want,* we strip ourselves of our power.

In other words, we bring to the table the part of us that came up with the error in the first place. We actually buy that the "impostor," the voice I call my "Inner Salieri," is where we'll find answers. If you saw the 1984 film *Amadeus,* you know all about Antonio Salieri, the Venetian composer, conductor, and director of the Hapsburg Opera who was intensely jealous of Mozart. In the film, made from the 1979 play of the same name, Salieri recognized the young composer's artistic gift and did everything he could to sabotage him. Just as my impostor delights in putting a roadblock between me and the higher forces.

The side effect of this ridiculous notion of limitation and separation is we go through life at half-mast. We actually live out the outdated Roman circus–like notion that we are weak and incapable of creating our lives.

Future generations will also consider it freakishly odd that we felt so guilty and didn't have the fun and joy to which we are entitled. They won't understand why we didn't revel in our creative powers. They'll puzzle, *They had this amazing gift, and they left it sitting in the corner, unwrapped.*

For what it's worth, future generations, I for one am doing my part now (even as we speak) to spend my day in unadulterated wonderment at all the world's blessings and miracles.

EXPERIMENT #1

THE BOOGIE-WOOGIE COROLLARY (*OR* THE IMPORTANCE OF NOT BEING EARNEST)

Meme: Events Happen; Therefore, I Feel Bad. (Aka "Wipe That Silly Grin Off Your Face.")

Worldview 2.0: Without Cultural Training, Joy Is My Natural State. In Fact, the More Fun I Have, the Better Life Works.

"When I went to school, they asked me what I wanted to be when I grew up. I wrote down 'happy.' They told me I didn't understand the assignment, and I told them they didn't understand life."
— JOHN LENNON, BRITISH MUSICIAN AND
FOUNDING MEMBER OF THE BEATLES

The Premise

In 2013, when writing an article about the best new African safaris, I learned a little-known fact about rhinos. Their eyesight sucks. Even at 15 feet away, they can't tell a human from a tree. So even though being charged by a rhino is high on the list of "things to fear in Africa," it's actually the least of your worries.

Rhinos, when startled, *do* begin running as fast as they can. And there's no disputing that four tons of snorting rhino barreling your way, most of it a devilishly large and very sharp horn, can appear rather troubling. But because rhinos are nearsighted, they're not really charging at you. They're simply running as fast as they possibly can in whatever direction they were pointed at the time they got spooked. All you really need to do is dive out of the way. That rhino will continue on the same trajectory until he finally wears himself out. Or realizes he's no longer in danger.

Your thoughts are like spooked rhinos. Once they get some momentum going, it's pretty hard to change their trajectory. Which is why my practice of getting up every morning and proclaiming "Something amazingly awesome is going to happen to me today" has revolutionized my life.

This simple practice takes what, ten seconds, but, if I had to choose, I'd forgo showering before giving up this this all-important daily ritual.

In this experiment, you're going to prove that by changing the momentum of the first few minutes of your day, you can rewrite the script of your life. By cutting off the feeding tube to the blah-blah soundtrack of negativity, you can begin to see real shifts in your day-to-day reality. By consciously starting your day focused on gratitude and joy, you'll find that your whole life will begin to sparkle.

What is the first thought that runs through your mind each morning? Is it something along the lines of *Woo-hoo! I'm awake! Time to party!*

Or is it more like, *Oh shit! Not again.*

Your first thoughts can become invincible tools. Especially if you let go of yesterday and feel the natural joy that comes when you're not regurgitating your normal script.

Because it's a vibrational universe and because thoughts become things, choosing happy thoughts is one of the most valuable gifts you can give yourself. The important thing is to milk those suckers (the good feelings) as long as you can.

Turn Your One-Lane Fun Channel into a Superhighway

"We actually get to decide right here, right now, to be miserable, or to be happy, no matter how complicated, fucked up or disagreeable our life may be."
— Chris McCombs, American fitness coach

Famous Harvard psychologist William James (yes, Henry's brother) liked to say humans are little but bundles of habit. Our habits of thought are so automatic that we rarely stop and think about the enormous role they play in shaping our expectations, our behavior, and yes, what shows up in our day-to-day lives.

We like to *think* we're composing new thoughts, coming up with new schemes, but most of us haven't had a new thought in 20 years. We filter the 400 billion bits of information that our brains receive each second through the lens of our culture's dominant paradigm. We let through a measly 2,000 bits, those that jibe with the neural pathways we set up as children.

Consequently, we march through life like robots, simply following programs that were unwittingly written into our neural pathways years ago. While some of these habits of thought serve us, the vast majority of them don't.

The good news is that our neural pathways, which scientists used to think were set for life, are actually malleable and can be changed. Which is why getting up every morning and looking for amazing awesomeness can radically transform your life. But just like working with any muscle, it takes practice.

Formula Broken

"Sometimes you just have to put on lip gloss and pretend to be psyched."
— MINDY KALING, INDIAN-AMERICAN ACTRESS AND AUTHOR

The prevailing wind of thought will tell you that happiness comes when your dreams and goals come true. But that's backwards. This popular paradigm goes something like this:

I'll be happy when my income increases. As soon as my son calls. Once a new President takes the Oval Office.

While no one except Eeyore or maybe Woody Allen would check the box "No" after the question "Do you want to be happy?" few of us believe we get to choose. We think it's a matter of fate, a roll of the dice.

Our judgments on what's fun and what isn't are pre-programmed tapes that run in an endless loop. And we march to them like Stalin's army. It never occurs to us to ask: "Is this really true?"

For example, is it really true that:

- Hanging with friends is fun. Cleaning the carpet isn't.

- Sleeping in is fun. Going to work isn't.

- Going to the movies is fun. Going to the dentist isn't.

You'll find very few people to disagree with these beliefs. Most of us cling to them like Billy Graham clings to God.

But making these kinds of judgment calls prevent us from enjoying large swaths of our lives. It's not "The Man" who is sticking it to you. It's the television evangelist in your head who constantly spoon-feeds you opinions and BS (belief systems) about what does and doesn't make you happy.

This slimy used-car salesman . . . er, I mean your mind . . . promotes a lot of lies. And in this experiment, you'll prove that by simply pulling your focus away from all your dissatisfaction and looking around at all the gifts you have, life can be simple and gloriously joyful. Yes, this is the gratitude chapter where you prove that happiness is an inside job.

Think Valuable Thoughts

"The world is only in the mind of its maker."
— *A Course in Miracles*

Who in their right mind would walk into a restaurant, take a look at the menu, and then order the dish they least desire?

Likewise, who would go shopping at Nordstrom and opt to carry the rack's ugliest outfit up to the sales counter?

Yet, that's what most of us do in our thinking, in our conversations. We focus on things we *don't* want to happen. We focus on the fear, on the negative, on the lack.

And those decisions have a much bigger impact on your life than one ugly dress or a dish you can't stand. You literally draw out from the universe whatever you focus upon. In other words, you get what you order. It's an unalterable law.

Some make the argument that they can't help what they think, that they have no control over the thoughts that pop into their minds. If you want to continue to believe that, it's your choice. But just so you know, that argument is a monster-size bucket of bull.

At every moment, we make the choice where we focus our energy. Always. One hundred percent of the time.

I'm not denying that our minds habitually return to worn-out grooves from the past and that it takes retraining to start a new habit, but we have the capacity to do it. Once we consciously focus on the superhigh frequencies of gratitude and joy.

In this experiment, we'll prove these superpowers not only make us feel good, but they energetically flush out mental and emotional blocks, remove resistance, and allow the FP's love and light to flow free and clear.

Waiting for Godot

"Spiritual practice is just training our minds towards reverence, like moving a potted plant to a sunny spot by the window."
— LANA MAREE, AMERICAN MUSICIAN

To start this experiment, please fill in the blanks of this very important goal-setting exercise:

- When _____ happens, I will be happy.

- As soon as _____, I will be happy.

- If _____ would only _____,
  I will be happy.

Now take said pen and mark out the first clause in each of those sentences.

Unless your pen ran out of ink, your new sentence should have these four words.

- I will be happy.

And that's your goal in this experiment. And the only thing necessary to have a full and complete life.

Choosing to be happy and saying thank you to whatever circumstances befall you is one of the most radical things you could ever do. But be forewarned: your life will never be the same. And you'll quickly come to realize there's very little in life that requires stoicism . . . unless, of course, the zombies show up, and then the rest of us can relax because there's already a whole army of really serious, really miserable people jonesing for a fight.

Never Have a Bad-Hair Day

"Be infinitely flexible and constantly amazed."
— Jason Kravitz, American actor

Not having a killer game of spades in my family is like not being able to moonwalk in Michael Jackson's family.

My family plays this innocuous card game every time we get together. And every single time, the same jokes come up. Mostly directed at me. How I'm not a suitable spades partner because I take too many chances. How it makes no sense why I would blow a huge lead by going nil when all I needed was 30 measly points.

For me, taking wicked risks and betting the whole she-bang is fun. I really enjoy sitting on the edge of my seat, wondering if I can make my bid. If I happen to win, it's a side benefit, but not at all why I play.

As my brother Bob likes to say, "Pam might not win, but nobody enjoys the game more. Nobody has more fun."

Which is what this experiment is about. Having fun. Turning your life into a party. Celebrating every gorgeous moment no matter what. Being grateful for it all—the cellulite, the Wal-Mart shoppers, the teen texters, Paris Hilton, the dandelions, the baby who smiled at you with her two new front teeth.

No Matter What

"Each day should be devoted to miracles."
— A COURSE IN MIRACLES

There's no question that, as a travel writer, I get to do a lot of cool things—meet medicine men from the Cook Islands, hang with wealthy people at five-star resorts, eat every meal beside the ocean—but it doesn't take that for me to have fun. My favorite recent example of this happened in 2012 when the world was scheduled to end.

Yes, I was invited to go to Belize to ring in the "end of the Mayan calendar" at Caracol, a Mayan jungle city still being excavated. The night I was supposed to pack for my 6 A.M. flight, my back went out. I wasn't able to go . . . at that time. So I lay in bed that first day in what some might describe as excruciating physical pain. I could barely get up to pee. But because of my commitment to fun and joy, I actually had a stellar day. I was so happy—really! I decided to have fun anyway. I look back at that day as very important to my spiritual growth because I realized this:

Our thoughts are the only things that separate us from nonstop happiness.

C'mon, Get Happy
(*or* The Perks of Brazen Gratitude)

"Sometimes your joy is the source of your smile, but sometimes your smile can be the source of your joy."
— THÍCH NHAT HANH, VIETNAMESE ZEN BUDDHIST MONK

Giving shout-outs to all the good in your life, more than just a soppy exercise, changes your brain and rewires your neural transmitters. When someone shows up on this planet with a grateful heart and eyes seeking only things for which to be thankful, that's exactly what she'll find: abundance aplenty.

Focusing on how lucky and blessed we are literally resculpts our brain. It increases our enthusiasm and lowers our stress. And if that weren't enough, think of all the good drugs (dopamine, serotonin, oxytocin) you miss out on when you're bitching.

We all showed up on Earth ready to have a good time. Toddlers, according to one research study, laugh 400 times a day. Adults laugh an average of four times. What happened?

Anecdotal Evidence

"Wearing a red rubber clown nose everywhere I go has changed my life."
— PATCH ADAMS, AMERICAN PHYSICIAN AND ACTIVIST

Patch Adams, the doctor whose life was made into a 1998 movie starring Robin Williams, says joy should be the platform on which a person launches his life.

"Being unhappy," he says, "is profoundly unhealthy. Happiness is not an ethical or a moral thing. It's a damned old choice. It is your right and no one can take it away."

Not only has Patch turned the medical profession upside down and sideways, but at the Gesundheit Institute, his innovative medical center in West Virginia, he takes the most expensive service in America—medical care—and gives it away free.

Patch, who calls himself a student of life, has spent most of his adulthood formulating a philosophy of happiness, about its importance and how it can be developed.

But it wasn't always that way. In fact, it was only after a two-week stint in a psychiatric ward that he found his true calling.

He was born an Army brat, moving every few years to new schools, new countries. When he was 16, his dad died suddenly, sending him into a grief-filled tailspin. His mom moved the family back to suburban Virginia, where he latched on to his uncle, a lawyer and an independent thinker in a society of conformists.

At school, he turned his grief into rage, writing scathing articles against segregation, war, and religious hypocrisy. He joined the jazz club, went to coffeehouses, shot pool, wrote long, sappy poetry. By the end of his senior year, Patch had ulcers. That was bad enough, but the next year, when he was a freshman in college, the uncle he'd adopted as a surrogate father committed suicide and Patch's girlfriend dumped him.

He dropped out of school and began obsessing about suicide. Every day he went to a cliff near the college and wrote epic poetry to the departed girlfriend. He composed heartrending sonnets, searching for just the right words that would convince her to see the error in her ways and take him back.

"If I had ever finished my outpouring, I would have jumped. Fortunately, I was too long-winded," Patch says.

Finally after one last unsuccessful plea to Donna, the girlfriend, he trudged six miles in the snow to his mother's doorstep.

"I'm trying to kill myself," he told his mother. "I need help."

His two-week stay at a locked ward in Fairfax, Virginia, was the turning point in his life. But it wasn't the doctors who helped him, he says, but his friends and family, and more important, his roommate, Rudy.

Rudy was a basket case. He'd had three wives and 15 jobs and told Patch long stories about his unfathomable loneliness. For the first time in his life, Patch empathized with another person. In fact, a lightbulb came on. Patch realized what he calls a great personal truth. Happiness is an intentional decision.

He devoted himself to learning everything he could about love, happiness, and friendship, and developing a joy-filled life. He read great works of literature. He devoured everything by Nikos Kazantzakis, Jean-Paul Sartre, Plato, Nietzsche, Walt Whitman, and many others. But his best bibliography, he says, grew out of his personal interactions with the people around him. He sought out happy families, examining how they nourish joy and happiness. He practiced friendliness by giving himself challenges—like calling 50 numbers in the phone book, seeing how long he could keep people on the phone. He'd ride elevators to see how may floors it took to get riders introduced and singings songs. Once, he went to a bar and refused to leave until he'd heard every patron's story.

Soon after leaving the hospital, he decided to pursue a career in medicine. Because of his hospitalization, admission officials delayed his admittance for nine months so he could "get himself together."

While waiting, he put his newfound happiness theories to work. He got a job in the file room for the Navy Federal Credit Union, hardly an upbeat atmosphere. Could he turn his filing job into something memorable? He and a co-worker decided to turn the joyless, dull job of filing into a happening. They drove to and from work wearing kids' aviator helmets with noisemakers. When people asked for files, they sang in a high-mass Gregorian chant: "Which file do you wa-ant?"

"Nurtured by levity and love, I blossomed. I defeated all my demons and became the person I am today," he says. "My self-confidence, love of wisdom, and desire to change the world were rooted in that brief period, when I climbed out of despair to rebirth."

More Anecdotal Evidence

"Drop the idea that you are Atlas carrying the world on your shoulders. The world would go on even without you. Don't take yourself so seriously."

— NORMAN VINCENT PEALE, AUTHOR OF THE POWER OF POSITIVE THINKING

Hobart Brown, a metal sculpture artist, was nominated for a Nobel Peace Prize in 1998. The reason? He has made happiness his occupation. He explains that by "following my heart, by doing what seems to be the most fun at the time and by not doing those things that weren't fun, I think I've lived a useful life."

Indeed. Not only has this zany artist put Ferndale, California, his home of several decades, on the map, but his invention of kinetic sculpture racing has inspired millions of people to take life less seriously. As he likes to say, "It seems to solve the problem of how to have fun as an adult."

When Hobart moved to Ferndale in 1962, this little dairy community of 2,500 was almost a ghost town. The glorious Victorian homes were selling for a song, and city fathers were thinking about tearing them down, replacing them with modern structures. A great dissension reigned between the farmers, who had been there since the late 1800s, and the artists, who were turning the cheap Victorians into funky studios.

Hobart's crazy brainstorm, which eventually turned into the Kinetic Grand Championship and features a kinetic sculpture race from Arcata to Ferndale, brings a quarter million people to town every Memorial Day weekend, pumps more than $2 million into the economy, and has totally healed the rift between the farmers and the artists.

Kinetic sculptures, in a nutshell, are works of art that move. Shaped like everything from giant bananas to two-ton dinosaurs to floating wheelchairs and 75-foot iguanas, these human-powered vehicles are pedaled, pushed, paddled, and pumped, Fred Flintstone–style. They're made from scrounged bicycle parts, discarded lawn-mower gears, painted septic tanks, old bathtubs, and anything else inventors can come up with. Each machine is a testament not only to childlike imagination and engineering genius but also to artistic ingenuity, camaraderie, and, well . . . insanity.

Hobart proves my point. One of the greatest ways to serve your fellow man is to figure out a way to enjoy yourself and to let people know that enjoying yourself is a good thing. When you decide to practice the attitude of happiness, boredom turns into exploration. Canceled flights turn into a party. Waiting in line becomes a great opportunity to meet new people. Vacuuming the floor is a ballet performed to Van

Morrison. And, of course, a rainy day calls for an indoor picnic with five kinds of cheese.

The Method

> *"It's always a good idea to sit at the fun table."*
> — ESTHER HICKS, FACILITATOR OF THE ENTITY ABRAHAM

If we really want to change the default setting in our little pea brains, the blueprint that erroneously points out that "life is hard, shit happens, and the glass is half-empty," you have to force new beliefs into your psyche.

Without us being consciously aware of it, our brains constantly send memos to our bodies that trigger our central nervous system, muscles, tendons, and joints. And then, much faster than most people answer our pressing texts, our bodies send memos back.

Luckily, your brain, thanks to what scientists call neuroplasticity, has the ability to pave new pathways. Your brain might look like a lump of protoplasm, but it's actually a network of connections. The ones most used become reinforced over time—like freeways. The weaker connections are still there, but as smaller back roads.

Using the techniques I recommend below heads those rote neural reactions off at the pass. These techniques provide an alternative entry to your natural state of joy that has fallen into a "woe is me" rut. They coax your nervous system into becoming your ally.

This experiment is a three-parter, designed with the sole intention of raising your fun antenna, which, if you're like most adults, has gotten a bit rusty.

Game 1:
The Right Side of the Bed
(*or* Start Your Day with a Laugh Track)

"When you rise in the morning, give thanks for the light, for your life, for your strength. Give thanks for your food and for the joy of living."
— Tecumseh, Native American leader

Okay, so this game involves music and a couple of easy movements that I call calisthenics for big-ass manifesting. Using the first five minutes of your day to feel good is like programming a destination into your GPS, like fixing your eye on the spot where you want your golf ball to land.

For the sake of experimentation, it's only necessary to do the little ritual I'm about to impart for the next three days. But my hope is you'll dig it enough to include it as a treasured part of your morning routine along with brushing your teeth and showering. Here's how it works:

LMFAO's "Party Rock Anthem" is now the theme song for your morning. Watch it on YouTube if you haven't already.

For the next three days, for a mere five minutes (c'mon, how easy it that?) you're going to throw the following feel-good party in your brain:

1. Listen to one or more of these songs, all easily accessible on your phone (maybe it could be your alarm?) or your computer:

- "Happy" by Pharrell Williams
- "What a Wonderful World" by Louis Armstrong
- "Best Day of My Life" by American Authors
- "I Believe I Can Fly" by R. Kelly

- "Three Little Birds" by Bob Marley
- "Celebration" by Kool and the Gang
- "I Feel Good" by James Brown
- "I Gotta Feeling" by Black Eyed Peas

2. Perform the following series of movements:

- Pump your fist in the air with complete glee. Repeat five times.

- Pretend you're a Latin American soccer player who just made a goal. In the finals. When the score was tied.

- Do the Harlem Shuffle on your way to the bathroom in the morning. Before you brush your teeth.

- Go outside and stretch your arms wide to salute the sun that comes up every day without you having to pay for it or ask it to.

Dancing to Pharrell Williams's "Happy" while brushing my teeth has literally resculpted my brain and lowered my stress level. As I mentioned earlier, dancing and pumping my fists in the air is better than *Breaking Bad*'s Walter White at furnishing me with a constant supply of happy drugs: dopamine, serotonin, and oxytocin, to name just a few.

Game 2:
Ask for Your Own Personal Cosmic Joke

Put in an order with the FP for something that will amuse you, something that makes you laugh out loud. Intend to be shown this "inside joke" within the next 72 hours, during the time frame of this experiment.

Game 3:
PDA for Your Mind

For the next three days, make a commitment to be grateful for everything that happens. And not just for things like, say, the turkey handprint your daughter brings home from school or your neighbor's blooming hydrangeas. If your mayonnaise jar falls out of the fridge while you're looking for the leftover chicken fried rice, say "Thank you!" If the po-po notices you're running late to work and gives you a citation to prove it, say thanks!

Extra-Credit Game

Take silly to the streets. In this game, you're going to be the person your mother always warned you about. This one isn't required for the experiment to work, but once you've mastered the first three games, you might agree with Patch Adams, who says, "I dove into the ocean of gratitude and I never found the shore."

For overachievers, your mission is to take your joy out into a public space. Create your own personal flash mob. Here are a few suggestions I've gathered into my own "fool box." No, that's not a typo. Instead of a tool box, I have a fool box with costumes, hats, and kazoos. As I'm sure Patch would agree, performing these acts tricks you into having fun.

- Enlist a friend to dress up with you in a weird costume. Go get coffee.

- Walk around downtown with a giant stuffed animal. I suggested this in *God Doesn't Have Bad Hair Days,* to prove how friendly people are, a discovery I made after bringing back a monstrous moose from a travel-writing gig in Montana. One reader offered to walk to my house all the way from New Jersey (I live in Kansas) with a four-foot teddy bear.

- Make a sign that says FREE HUGS! Take it to a shopping mall downtown and make good on your offer.

- Do some reverse panhandling. I learned this trick from Rob Brezsny, the horoscope guy, who ran for office as the nation's first Fool Czar. It's like a drug czar, only instead of educating the nation on the hazards of drugs, his Cabinet position has the mission of teaching us how dangerous it is to take everything so seriously. At least once a year, he stands on an exit ramp holding $5 bills and a cardboard sign that says: I NEED TO GIVE. PLEASE TAKE MY MONEY.

- Sing out loud in the grocery store.

Lab Report Sheet

The Corollary: The Boogie-Woogie Corollary

The Theory: The more fun I have, the better life works.

The Question: Is it possible that joy is my natural state? That I can be happy even without the job, the relationship, the bank balance I want?

The Hypothesis: If I cut off the feeding tube to my ongoing litany of problems and doom, I will feel more joy and thus open channels of goodness.

Time Required: 72 hours

Today's Date: _____ **Time:** _____

The Approach: I will follow the easy steps outlined by Pam Grout first thing every morning. I will listen to the songs and perform the bad-ass calisthenics. I will record how I feel at the start and how I feel at the end.

I will also, no matter what happens in the next three days, commit to saying, "That's amazing!" And I will ask the universe for my own inside cosmic joke.

How I feel right now (at the beginning of the experiment):

_____

How I feel in three days: _____

Research Notes: _____

_____

_____

◼ ◼ ◼

"I want a life that sizzles and pops and makes me laugh out loud. . . . I want my everyday to make God belly laugh, glad that he gave life to someone who loves the gift."

— SHAUNA NIEQUIST, AUTHOR OF *COLD TANGERINES*

Raining Cats and Blogs

Use This Year's 525,600 Minutes to
Write a Different Story on Your Etch-a-Sketch

You've heard it a million times: George Santayana's famous line "Those who cannot remember the past are condemned to repeat it."

I'd like to take this opportunity to point out that it is *only* our remembrance of the past that condemns us to repeat it. If we got up every morning with a completely clean Etch-a-Sketch, with not an iota of an idea of how so-and-so reacts or which dangerous road we think our world is heading on or even what the status of our financial situation is, we would be free to write a brand-new story.

We are the creators of our reality, but instead of using this oh-so-awesome gift, we have the tendency to create our reality based on the past. We get up each day and focus on the same-ole, same-ole we created yesterday.

What's even worse is yesterday's same-ole, same-ole is filtered through our fears and illusions so the past we're "condemned to repeat" isn't even accurate.

I think it's also important to remind you that you are the captain of your thoughts, the boss of your Etch-a-Sketch, and that, at any time, you can throw yesterday's memories overboard. You can use your will to create a brand-new reality. I mean, starting from scratch.

Nobody's forcing you to focus on anything. You get to choose.

Why write the same old soap opera? Why assume today is going to be just like yesterday? Do you really know for certain that your boss is an a-hole? That your partner is going to defy your needs? What if they only act like that because that's what you draw out of them with old expectations? Why not decide right now to draw out a more pleasing reality. You get to choose. Always!

The main thesis of *A Course in Miracles* boils down to forgiveness, which doesn't mean forgiving someone for yesterday's wrong. It means letting yesterday go and not making the assumption that the blessed *now* will be a rerun.

There's no reason it has to be except your decision to "remember the past."

EXPERIMENT #2

THE RED PILL COROLLARY (*OR* A QUICK REFRESHER COURSE)

Meme: Life Happens to Me.

Worldview 2.0: Life Emanates from Me.

"Life doesn't come at you. It comes from you."
—JASON MRAZ, AMERICAN MUSICIAN

The Premise

In the movie *The Matrix*, the protagonist, Neo, is given a choice. He can either (a) take the blue pill and remain unaware of his own power or (b) take the red pill and discover reality without the preprogrammed scripts.

In this experiment, you get another chance to take the red pill.

In *E-Squared,* I offered a whole medicine chest of red pills, most of which were gleefully swallowed. As the dispenser of such meds, I quickly learned, as I explained in Chapter 3, that you can't write a book like this without being inundated with stories, signs, and synchronicities.

I've been introduced to all sorts of new literature, including a fabulous book by astrophysicist Bernard Haisch that was literally dropped in my lap by a prosecuting attorney from nearby Wichita, who treated me to a lovely two-hour al fresco lunch and said, "Here. Read this." Haisch's book *The God Theory* reinforces many of my ideas and proposes that "ultimately it is consciousness that is the origin of matter, energy, and the laws of nature." As Haisch says, "The purpose of our universe is for God to experience his potential."

So in honor of giving God a real bang-up experience, filled with celebration and joy and magnificent fun, this experiment is a corollary to the Volkswagen Jetta Principle, where readers draw specific things into their awareness. Like its predecessor, it is intended to prove that your thoughts, feelings, and beliefs are reproduced in the events around you, events that we used to call coincidence or synchronicity.

The Universe Never Stops Courting You

"Let's get one thing clear right now, shall we? . . . Ideas seem to come quite literally from nowhere, sailing at you right out of the empty sky. . . . Your job isn't to find these ideas but to recognize them when they show up."

— STEPHEN KING, AMERICAN AUTHOR

H&R Block ran a brilliant ad campaign during the 2014 tax season. The tagline "Get your billion back, America" showed a concession worker dropping $500 on every seat in a giant football stadium. The idea was that those of us doing our own taxes were missing out on big breaks and loads of money. In other words, we're cheating ourselves out of what's rightfully ours.

That's what this experiment is about.

Only instead of cheating ourselves out of billions of dollars, we humans are cheating ourselves out of valuable information and signs that are trying their damnedest to get our attention. We're leaving on the table massive amounts of intel that could help steer our lives. By living in our one-dimensional reality, by believing in our teardrop-size viewfinder, by doing all our computations by ourselves, we miss out on the largesse of the universe.

Use it or lose it.

That oft-repeated adage usually refers to the body ("I'd love to run that 10K next week, but I haven't even put on my tennis shoes in two years") or the mind ("I used to be fluent in Arabic, but my friend who I spoke it with moved back to Saudi and now I can't even remember how to say thank you"). But "use it or lose it" is just as true of intuition, of accessing the higher realms that are an important, if undervalued, part of our inheritance.

We have friends in high places, folks. We are connected to this giant universal love energy, this field that hooks us up to everything we could ever need. The problem is we're not paying attention. Every moment, we are offered valuable information, really clear signposts, and 24-7 guidance, but by relying instead on our barely conscious minds, we've shrunk this mind-blowing, multidimensional universe into a shoebox.

Climbing Out Is No More Difficult
Than Learning to Play Chess

"I am larger, better than I thought; I did not know I held so much goodness."
— Walt Whitman, American poet and essayist

To access these other dimensions that, as I said, are flying around the ethers like text messages is a simple matter of attention, a simple decision to enlarge what you notice. As you now know, your brain, specifically the prefrontal cortex, engineers reality. It crunches and tags data, filters and constructs information according to the default programming you've set up. This programming decides what to let in, what to suppress, and what to believe is possible. Much from the higher, more subtle energy realms ends up getting deleted, while the regularly scheduled programs—sensations in our bodies, nearby material things—get enhanced and directed to center stage.

Beyond the frequency range of our five senses is a magnitude of information, a whole spectrum of energy frequencies that, by treating like door-knocking evangelists, we completely miss. To ignore the nonvisible frequencies just because we can't tango with them is to miss out on all sorts of guidance and comfort. We can't see microwaves or infrared waves either, but we certainly don't snub them when last night's leftovers need warming up or when the Lifetime movie we're watching gets too maudlin. By opening our minds and our consciousness, by out-and-out demanding guidance and expecting signs, we can tap into a whole new river of possibility.

Bernie Siegel, M.D., the best-selling author of *Love, Medicine & Miracles,* claims to get regular and dependable guidance from the unseen realm. He finds cures, solutions, and information that some might think impossible. Why? Because he's open to atypical spaces of consciousness. He even uses this Divine Broadcast for making decisions in his personal life. A few years ago when trying to decide whether or not to run a marathon, he asked for a sign. Within a day, he found 26 pennies, the number of *miles* in a marathon.

Who Needs a Crystal Ball?

"You owe it to yourself to do something truly remarkable with your life."

— HAND-PRINTED SIGN SEEN ON THE PIANO OF A
TRAVELING MUSICIAN IN QUEBEC CITY

Not only is the FP sending you paper airplanes with messages, but it's also constantly inviting you to do something remarkable with your life. The universe has been dropping hints for years.

At last count, the 2002 novel *The Secret Life of Bees* had sold six million copies; had been translated into 35 languages; and was made into a movie starring Queen Latifah, Alicia Keys, and Dakota Fanning. But it would never have been written if its author, Sue Monk Kidd, hadn't been bold and reckless enough to ask for what she wanted and to follow the bread crumbs that led there.

In 1993, at a convent in Palianis on the Greek island of Crete, Kidd bowed before a dark-faced icon of the Virgin Mary. She humbly asked for the courage to become a novelist. She always knew she wanted to write, even though her fear of making a decent living at it convinced her to get a nursing degree and work as an RN. Until that day when she dared utter her dream out loud to the icon hanging from a gnarly tree branch, she mainly wrote inspirational nonfiction, documenting stories from her life with her husband, Sandy, and her two kids.

She returned from Greece and wrote a first chapter about a girl whose bedroom wall is full of bees. She took it to a writer's conference, where the professor who was teaching there called it "interesting, but with small potential." Even though she was being nudged to write a book, she turned that chapter into a short story and promptly forgot about it. Except not really.

It percolated in her mind for six years. Six years and a couple of nonfiction books later, she was in the Mediterranean again, this time on a postgraduation trip with her daughter Ann. Only now she was approaching menopause and her unrequited dream of being a novelist was still banging around inside her heart, still trying to make its presence known. At Ephesus, in an olive grove outside the little home where Mary once lived, she decided to ask again.

As she wondered in her memoir, *Traveling with Pomegranates*, "When we send prayers into the universe, are they heard? Can they change anything? Or are our supplications a form of magical thinking?"

It had been a long while since she'd made a concrete petition, but she asked again about the novel. She wanted guidance, a clear sign.

No sooner did she leave the little prayer chapel to rejoin her daughter than a bee landed on her left shoulder. Ann reached reflexively to wave it away, but Sue put out her hand, shaking her head, as if to say, "No. It's a bee. A *bee*."

They walked down the hill, beside the spring with holy water. The bee held its ground, rode back to the tour bus on Sue's shoulder.

"What's with this bee?" Ann said, genuinely affected. "It's like it has adopted you."

"It's telling me I'm about to go home and finish up that novel I started six years ago," Sue said.

Down the Rabbit Hole

"Once we shift our perspective, we can never turn back. We stand poised like a deer sniffing the wind—alive. With this new way of looking inward for direction, watching for tiny clues, we realize that not only can we make a difference, but this is the real reason we are here."
— CAROL ADRIENNE, CO-AUTHOR OF *THE TENTH INSIGHT*

Once you find out about the power of your thoughts and consciousness, there is no turning back. You can't really *undrink* the Kool-Aid.

You can choose not to use this information, you can be like Cypher in *The Matrix,* who told Morpheus to shove that red pill right up his ass, but you can never forget. And, in fact, you can never "not use" it. You just do it unconsciously, creating your life with society's default setting, reinforcing the historical tale of woe.

Where our story departs Hollywood is that in real life, you get unlimited chances to choose the red pill. Opportunities, like whiskers, keep coming back.

People mistakenly worry there's a time limit for their good, a sell-by date. They fret that they missed their chance back in 1986 or that time they turned down so-and-so. The chance to create your good reappears over and over every moment. You can't really miss the boat, because there's another one right behind it.

Synchronicity, Patterns, and Bigger Realities
(*or* A Rose by Any Other Name)

"Our ability to shape energy is like breathing.
We do it all the time without even realizing it."

— Damien Echols, former inmate, current poet, and spiritual teacher

In her book *Tiny Beautiful Things*, Cheryl Strayed, posing as Dear Sugar, tells a story of hiking in New Mexico. She was alone and had been for several hours. She turned a bend and suddenly ran into another solo hiker who at that exact moment had run into yet another lone hiker. The three of them laughed, began talking, and discovered that all three of them had the same birthday, in three consecutive years.

The brilliant European journalist Arthur Koestler told the story of a Frenchman who, when he was a young boy in Orléans, was given a plum pudding by a visitor to his parents' home. The visitor, Michael de Fortgibu, made almost as much of an impression on the young Frenchman as the plum pudding. Several years later, he was dining in Paris and after noticing plum pudding on the menu, ordered it only to be told by the waiter that he'd just sold the last piece. The waiter pointed to the gentleman on the other side of the restaurant who had ordered it. It was none other than Michael de Fortgibu, whom the young Frenchman hadn't seen since that night at his parents' home.

Many years later, the Frenchman was at a dinner party where plum pudding was being served. Just as he was recounting the remarkable story of ordering plum pudding and running into de Fortgibu at the Paris restaurant, there was a knock at the door. In walked a very old, frail, and frazzled Michael de Fortgibu. He had been invited to another dinner party and had come to the wrong address.

Coincidence, rather than being some weird anomaly spit out by what Dr. John Lilly called "The Cosmic Coincidence Control Center," is actually evidence of the field of infinite potentiality to which we are all connected. It is the scientific reason the Volkswagen Jetta Principle ("You impact the field and draw from it according to your beliefs and expectations") is so effective.

Carl Jung, the first to coin the term *synchronicity,* believed these uncanny coincidences are a glimpse into the underlying order of the universe. The serendipity of my bumping into another exchange student from Kansas in the library at the University of Sydney the one time I was there (I was studying at Macquarie University on the other side of town) or running into my aunt and uncle whom I hadn't seen in five years at a restaurant in Juárez, Mexico, are what Jung described as the "acausal connecting principle" that links mind and matter.

His theory was that when a strong need arises in the psyche, the underlying connectedness manifests itself to come to our aid. I'd like to suggest that even times when there isn't a strong need, the underlying connectedness is working, sending us signs and messages and trying to get through. Worldview 2.0 suggests that we live in a world more intricately and holistically organized than we ever previously supposed.

The more we allow ourselves to be aware of this connection to this always-flowing field of infinite potentiality, the more this dance of energy plays out in our favor. Many of us would rather persist in "feeling separate" than acknowledge that the universe works nonstop to bestow blessings, to pour out love, to provide us with all our needs.

Take Shelley, a reader who sent me this story. She was vacationing in Paris, resting her sore feet on a bench at Notre Dame. The one pair of shoes she'd packed for her Parisian adventure were not a good fit and her throbbing tootsies were making sure she knew it. Because she was touring Europe on the $20-a-day plan, she had no extra moola for a new pair of shoes. Suddenly, she got an intuitive hit to get up, walk out of the church, and turn left. A few more turns led her to a trash can upon which sat a brand-new pair of black boots, unworn, in her exact size.

She was virtually handed the boots by the universe.

Most of us set up a framework of beliefs to explain this intricate and holistically organized field that brings "coincidences" and "synchronicity" into our awareness. For some of us, it's angels who provide the nod to turn right when going straight would end in disaster. Or we call the book that falls off the shelf at the library fate or pure dumb luck. Others, as the old saying goes, believe "coincidence is God's wish to remain anonymous."

What you call it doesn't matter. That you use it matters more than anything.

Anecdotal Evidence

"I've been a manifesting super freak for over 20 years."
— HONORÉE CORDER, AUTHOR OF THE
SUCCESSFUL SINGLE MOM SERIES

Dr. Joe Dispenza, a chiropractor with a background in neurology, brain function, and neuroscience, knows that creating a particular reality is a simple matter of focusing your mind. Unlike many parents who dissuade their children from believing in fairy tales, who quickly teach "God" out of them, Dispenza taught his kids about the infinite power of the universe. He told them they could have anything they wanted.

Anything they were willing to convince their minds and bodies was true.

One summer, after his 15-year-old daughter manifested a starring role in a YouTube video that went viral, he asked her, "So what's next? What do you want to create now?"

She didn't have to think about it. "I want an unlimited shopping spree."

Again, most parents would have said something like, "When pigs fly!" but Dispenza nodded and said, "Okay, here's what you do. You have to get very clear in your mind what it would look like to have the most amazing shopping spree of your life. You need to practice this every day. And when you get up from meditating about this awesome shopping spree, you can't be the same person who sat down. You have to get up feeling as if you've just shopped your brains out."

"No problem, Dad," she said, completely ignoring his scholarly lecture about changing the circuitry in her brain, about emotionally conditioning her body to believe that her shopping spree had already been accomplished.

A month or two later, Dr. Dispenza was in Washington, D.C., in a taxi headed to a lecture. He got a phone call.

"Dad, guess what?" His daughter was breathless.

"Settle down, honey. Tell me what happened."

"I just got my shopping spree."

Turns out, she was shopping with a friend in Santa Monica, California. They were riffling through the racks in their favorite store when a man they'd never seen came up and asked her friend if she was Sam Barelli's daughter.

Her friend nodded, not quite sure what to think about this over-friendly stranger.

"The reason I'm asking is because Sam did me a huge favor a few months ago and I've been looking for a way to pay him back."

He reached into his pocket and handed them a company credit card. "I'd like to give this to you girls for the afternoon. Take it and have fun."

"Okay," Dispenza said. "I have to ask. How much?"

"Seven thousand five hundreds dollars," she said. "But that's not even the best part. The best part is how much fun it was, even more than I imagined. And Dad? I created this whole thing with my mind."

More Anecdotal Evidence

"You play on the stage created by your thoughts."
— DR. KIRBY SURPRISE, AMERICAN PSYCHOLOGIST

During the promotional campaign for *E-Squared,* I was introduced to a book called *The Cosmic Ordering Service.* Dr. Leslie Wells, a chiropractor who interviewed me on her radio show, told me she'd been practicing these principles for many years. In fact, she claimed to have met the love of her life by putting in a "cosmic order."

Intrigued, I had to ask (hey, I'm a journalist), and she explained that cosmic ordering is a simple process where you place an order with the universe for whatever you'd like— a new job, a new car, or in Dr. Leslie's case, a husband. It's much like setting an intention, in *E-Squared*-speak.

Barbel Mohr, the German author who came up with the process, instructed folks to simply write down their desire, request a delivery date, and let the universe do the rest. She called it a cosmic mail-order service, similar to ordering the latest bestseller from Amazon. Except there's no money involved. I like that in a process.

Cosmic ordering became the rage in England after former BBC broadcaster Noel Edmonds (he's the Larry King of

London) credited Mohr's book, given to him by his reflexologist, with turning his career around. His smash hit, *Deal or No Deal,* was the direct result of putting in an order with the universe, as were a home in southern France and his new wife. In fact, it was quite fashionable at that time for many winners on British reality shows to claim they'd put in a cosmic order.

Mohr, who went on to write several books about cosmic ordering before her death in 2010, didn't start out as a believer. In fact, she placed her first "order" simply to shut up a friend who wouldn't stop blathering on about positive thinking. Mohr, who was single at the time, finally said, "You mean to tell me I could find a perfect partner just by thinking positively? I'll take that bet."

So she wrote down the qualities she wanted in a guy, ceremoniously placed her "order," set a delivery date, and forgot all about it.

On the very day of her requested delivery, a guy with every single quality she'd ordered asked her out on a date. She was so floored that, after ponying up the ante to her friend, she went on to order (and eventually receive) her dream job, all the money she could spend, and a castle in which to live and work.

As she said, "We're all ordering all the time anyway—it's just that most of the time it's unconscious."

The Method

> *"These weren't the only hints that*
> *I was about to emigrate to a new universe."*
> — SUE MONK KIDD, AUTHOR OF *THE SECRET LIFE OF BEES*

This experiment is a refresher course, a warm-up to get those manifesting muscles back in shape, and a reminder that you get out of life whatever you're looking for. Physicists call this web of connection the zero point field (what I call the field of infinite potentiality, or the FP) and claim that, within it, every possibility exists.

For the next 72 hours, you are going to actively look for the following eight "possibilities." Just keep your eyes open and make the intention to draw them into your conscious awareness. The idea is that once you've "ordered them" from the universe, they'll show up exactly as ordered. And just like you never doubt that Amazon will deliver the new *Call of Duty* videogame to your doorstep, simply trust that the following eight things are rushing your way:

- A belly laugh
- A toy from your childhood
- Your favorite song from high school
- The number 222
- A beach ball
- A senior citizen in a fashionable hat
- A smile from a baby
- A billboard with a message for you

Think of it as a scavenger hunt, which was my favorite childhood game. And since childlike wonder and playing around are the elixir of manifestation, I'm going to spice this up by offering a manifestation prize pack with copies of all the books listed on page 220. These Hay House Titles of Related Interest will go to the reader who sends the best photographs of all eight things to my website, www.pamgrout.com.

And if you really want to make it fun, pick up some Red Hots or red jelly beans (for taking the "red pill"), a suggestion

I got from a wonderful reader named Mary Salyars. She keeps red jelly beans in a glass jar on her table, and every time she has one of those "moments," she pops one as a sweet reminder to choose a different reality.

Lab Report Sheet

The Corollary: The Red Pill Corollary

The Theory: My beliefs and expectations impact what I draw from the field of potentiality.

The Question: Is it possible I only see what I expect to see?

The Hypothesis: If I decide to look for the eight things listed below, I will find them.

Time Required: 72 hours

Today's Date: _____ **Time:** _____

The Approach: If this experiment holds water, it means that the world out there reflects what I expect to see. In the next three days, I am going to look for and check off the following eight things:

- A belly laugh _____
- A toy from your childhood _____
- Your favorite song from high school _____
- The number 222 _____
- A beach ball _____
- A senior citizen in a fashionable hat _____
- A smile from a baby _____
- A billboard with a message for you _____

Research Notes: _____

_____

_____

"The more you look for synchronicity, the more magical your life becomes. You are the magician that makes the grass green."

— ROBERT ANTON WILSON, AMERICAN AUTHOR

Raining Cats and Blogs

Do Your Beliefs Block the Flow
of the World's Limitless Abundance?

"If you want to find the secrets of the universe, think in terms of energy, frequency and vibration."
— Nikola Tesla, Serbian-American inventor

I'm more or less illiterate when it comes to anything electrical. I know what a plug looks like, and I know how to attach it to a wall socket. Beyond that, I draw a blank.

But there's a device used in electronics that provides a good metaphor for understanding why some intentions are so easy to manifest and why others seem darned near impossible. The device is called a resistor, and basically (all you electricians out there, please forgive my simplistic explanation) what it does is reduce the amount of electrical current flowing through a circuit. Resistors limit the number of electrons that can flow past a given point at any one time.

Our beliefs about ourselves and about the way the world works serve as resistors, blocking the flow of the world's limitless abundance. Our beliefs are the brakes that stop the natural, always-flowing current of good.

Let me give you an example. Most people believe money is limited and hard to come by. That's a resistor. On the other hand, they don't believe health or intelligence is limited. Just because I'm healthy doesn't mean you can't be healthy, too. Stephen Hawking's brilliant intellect doesn't prevent Matt Groening and Steven Spielberg from using their brainpower.

But when it comes to abundance, the belief there's only so much to go around is a big fat resistor, much better at blocking the flow than tungsten, carbon, and other popular resistors. The other family-size resistor is believing you know how to best accomplish a particular goal. Let's take traveling, a popular intention for many. Most people I talk to believe the best way to become a world traveler is to get a job so they can accumulate enough money and vacation time to visit, say, Cape Town or Monte Carlo or even Denver, Colorado.

I, on the other hand, had no expectations one way or another. I knew I had a burning desire to travel, but I had nary a clue how to make that happen. What I did have is the wherewithal to acknowledge I had no clue. It was abundantly clear to me that if I was going to jet around the world, my *only* option was to give it up to the universe. I let it go completely, trusting that the universe was a heck of a lot smarter and more abundant than I was.

Instead of following the "accepted path" of slaving away and accumulating money and vacation time, I now travel for free. The universe led me into travel writing, an occupation I'm not even sure I knew existed when I first made the declaration that I wanted to be a world traveler.

Money? Who needs money?

In the world of electronics, resistors sometimes come in handy (they can create heat and light), but for me, who longs for a life of ease and grace, I prefer to keep the flow as wide-open as I possibly can.

EXPERIMENT #3

THE SIMON COWELL COROLLARY (*OR* WHY YOU'RE NOT CAPABLE OF JUDGING ANYTHING)

Meme: My Job Is to Judge Between Right and Wrong, Black and White.

Worldview 2.0: Nothing Is Absolute; Only My Thinking Makes It So.

"Man has always been his own most vexing problem."
— REINHOLD NIEBUHR, AMERICAN THEOLOGIAN

The Premise

I named this experiment after the famous *American Idol* judge, whom *TV Guide* named to their list of "Nastiest Villains of All Time," because when we vigilantly cast scores on right and wrong, good and bad, we lose out; we strangle our energy.

I know making judgments seems necessary for fully understanding life. But "understanding things" is really a synonym for taking away their power. Once you start labeling— *This is an oak tree. That is a juvenile delinquent. That thing over there is a couch*—all other possibilities are cut off at the knees, severed like the head in *The Godfather.* That oak tree might be the home for a squirrel or a hiding spot in hide-and-seek, that juvenile delinquent might be a brilliant artist, that couch could be a bed or a fort for your six-year-old. Once we figure everything out, we stop looking for anything else.

Above all else, this experiment examines the old-school belief in absolute reality. Since we've only got three days, let's leave potential absolutes like the cosmos, higher deities, and original thought to the geniuses, and we'll examine the "absolutes" we believe about ourselves.

For example, is it absolute reality you're not photogenic or lucky in love? Is it absolute reality you don't make enough money or could never leave your loveless relationship? We all have them: beliefs we cling to and invest in no matter what the evidence.

One of my "absolutes" used to be "I'm not a very good public speaker. I'm not comfortable getting up on a stage in front of an audience." I told this story over and over again. It became a mantra to me. Every one of my friends has heard this poor woe-is-me story a thousand times. But it's not any more true than the flip side, where I'm a marvelous, confident, inspiring speaker.

In the quantum world, in the field of infinite potentiality, no reality is truer than any other. There's no such thing as absolutes, no definitive truth. Defining myself as an inexperienced speaker is just one of many probabilities. An equally valid probability is that I'm a talented speaker. It's every bit as true. Even if, up until now, I've pulled out and nursed another probability I've been proclaiming like a broken record.

If I examined it with the help of Sigmund Freud, I could probably find a lot of reasons for repeating my "I'm not a good speaker" mantra. One, I got sympathy and pats on the back. Whenever I said it (again, anytime the subject came up), my friends dutifully repeated their rote lines.

"But Pam," they'd say, "you're usually so entertaining. So funny. How could you not be a great speaker?"

"More. More," I was always tempted to say.

So my mantra reaped brownie points. And attention and a good excuse for avoiding something I actually longed to do.

But every time I repeated these boring, rote put-downs, I added bulk to that particular reality. I filled the bucket of that probability, making it heavier and heavier to carry. So the quicker I set down that particular "bucket of facts," the quicker I began enjoying the reality of being a confident public speaker.

Absolute Reality . . . Not So Much

"You can suffer, but only from false beliefs."
— Michele Longo O'Donnell, American author

It's a common delusion that there are good guys and bad guys, those wearing white hats and those who deserve to be tied to the railroad tracks. This game of right-and-wrong, win-or-lose, me-or-you has reached pandemic proportions.

By dividing and labeling everything, we automatically diminish our possibilities by a whopping 50 percent. By believing there's such a thing as one right answer, we lose half our options, half our personal freedom, half our energy.

We also end up with a lot more rules.

The invisible, all-powerful energy force gets sliced and diced, classified and categorized, until its juice, its unlimited mojo, gets sucked right out of it. By playing on this battlefield, we send the force that shapes and molds our lives out to scout for the small and the piteous. Our constant judgments and game-day analyses erect a thick curtain between us and the field of infinite potentiality.

The mental gymnastics it takes to play this either-or game sets up resistance, causes us to blame others, and trains us to see everything as a problem. It turns literally everything in our lives into our enemy. Even our own bodies, which we fully expect (although we do everything we possibly can to postpone it) to eventually decay, get sick, and rot away.

Worldview 1.0 is based on the belief that everything is out to get us: the environment, our politicians, our food, our bodies (which we examine regularly for breakdowns in yearly checkups), other countries, even our lovers, whom we've been warned to examine for signs that he's just not that into us.

Every news report, every commission, every political speech, every self-help book is based on our unending fascination with "what's wrong." We take pills, we buy energy drinks, we twist ourselves into yoga poses, we chant, we meditate, we pray to some nebulous deity in a fruitless search to correct all the wrong in our lives. Or the wrong we've been warned is coming.

History books are filled with lurid recountings of war, famine, and political unrest. As Patch Adams, the American doctor who was the inspiration for the eponymous movie, once wisely asked, "Where's the party chapter?"

We Only See What We've Been Taught to See

"Normal is not something to aspire to, it's something to get away from."
— JODIE FOSTER, AMERICAN ACTRESS

Could it be that by treating, analyzing, and working so diligently to annihilate all these problems, we give them power to govern us? Is it possible that exercising such extreme efforts to "avoid" our inevitable demise actually facilitates the very demise we're hoping to avert?

What this experiment suggests is that it is our misplaced fear itself that powers and drives the hysteria. And that our 5,000 years of education on the reign of lack, limitation, and gloom has blinded us to the simple, unchanging goodness that's forever on our side.

During the next 72 hours, I'm going to ask you to put down your dukes, to take off your armor and expect to catch a glimpse of the life-sustaining energy that flows through you, that takes care of you, that provides for every one of your needs.

What's Your Story, Morning Glory?

"Martin Luther King, Jr., never said, 'I have a complaint.'"
— MICHAEL BERNARD BECKWITH, AMERICAN AUTHOR AND PASTOR

We all have stories. Like the Brothers Grimm, we retell these stories to anyone who will listen.

- "I have trouble sleeping."
- "I hate to exercise."
- "I've never been organized."

But these stories are not any more true (except to the degree you've repeated them and made them your personal calling card) than are their opposites. Than a whole palette of other stories. Some of our stories serve us. For example, another one of my stories (and I choose to stick with this one) is that I'm a brilliant writer. Adding weight to that story and repeating it to myself has enabled me to write 17 books. It's enabled me to have a career doing what I love.

By repeating a story over and over again, we create neural pathways in the brain that reinforce that reality.

Life Is Multiple Choice

"Quantum junction. Get in both lanes."
— Street sign, shared on Facebook

Reality is radically different depending on whom you talk to. Some people smoke their entire lives and never get lung cancer. Some people consume endless calories, gobble gluten and every other "harmful thing," and still have bodies like Kate Moss. Some people read books like this and produce no results.

I learned about the absence of a cut-and-dried reality when I was in journalism school. My Reporting I teacher, in her zest to provide us with real-life experience, set up "news events" for us budding reporters to report. Even though the first credo of journalism is objectivity and we're taught that bias of any kind is an unwelcome guest, the reports we filed were as different as the opinions of Barack Obama and Vladimir Putin.

I'd think, *Did you really see the same event I just saw?*

There's No One Right Answer

"If reality differs from person to person, can we speak of reality singular, or shouldn't we really be talking about plural realities? And if there are plural realities, are some more true . . . than others?"

— PHILIP K. DICK, AMERICAN SCIENCE-FICTION WRITER

A belief is only a thought we continue to think over and over again. We decide how things are and proceed to do everything we can to prove that conclusion. What if, instead of searching so hard for the right answer, we simply admit there's no universal anything.

By giving up the notion of absolute reality, we no longer have to defend our positions or cast about aimlessly for someone to blame. Once we quit trying to squish life into our neat little box of right and wrong, we can use this potential to create whatever we want.

Choosing not to judge often seems uncomfortable. Everything in Worldview 1.0 screams the importance of finding *the* one: the one right partner, the one right career, the one right lifestyle. Not only does this put tremendous pressure on us (*OMG, what if I get it wrong? What if I pick the wrong answer?*), but it's also patently false. In the quantum soup, there are millions of right answers.

When we believe there's but one right answer, we become indignant at those who have obviously chosen the wrong answer. Once we realize there are different right answers for everyone, we can back off on the judgment, be more playful, more fluid, more open to the boisterous palette of possibilities.

Anecdotal Evidence

"Change but your mind on what you want to see, and all the world must change accordingly."
—*A Course in Miracles*

At 25, Michele Longo O'Donnell, the author of *Of Monkeys and Dragons,* was an RN, working at one of the first pediatric intensive care units in the nation. She was married to a Vietnam Marine vet, had a two-year-old daughter, and was pregnant with her second child. Because she'd had her withered left kidney removed when she was younger, docs thought her right kidney was overloaded and decided to induce birth by giving her a drug to begin labor.

A mistake in the calculation of her due date caused her daughter Lara to be born at seven months, weighing a mere two and a half pounds. Twenty-four hours after the IV drip began, doctors whisked away the tiny purple baby who made no movement, no sound. She was diagnosed with what's known as hyaline membrane disease. She was unable to take in air or keep her lungs inflated. During the first night, she had five cardiac arrests. Even with 100 percent oxygen being pumped into her lungs, she was still not getting enough to supply her kidneys and brain. Back in 1970, babies in this condition did not survive.

But when the senior resident came in the next morning asking permission to stop treatment, something inside Michele told her it would all be okay. Even though she knew, as a six-year nurse, that severe mental retardation was the outcome of oxygen deprivation, she refused to give permission to pull the plug.

"It was as if there were two people living inside me. One was an emotional wreck, my usual hyper-frightened self. That one smoked myself sick. Called the lab for results on her blood work every hour. When I snuck down to see her, her arms were flailing in the air as she struggled to get air into her lungs," she said.

Yet, there was another self with a deep, underlying conviction in the quantum probability that "everything was going to be all right."

Her husband abandoned her two days later, and for two long years, after Lara was finally released from the ICU, O'Donnell pieced together a life, never once "owning" the probability of mental retardation or letting go of the probability that healing was still possible.

"I felt deep within me that it was critical that I not give permission for this thing to be part of our lives. It may be what we had to deal with, but it was not going to be our identity," she said.

Of course, you must deal with problems if they arise. But it's unnecessary to let them become your whole identify. No matter how it may look, you are still whole and complete and intact. To focus on the problem is to subconsciously cling to it, never allowing for the possibility of release. There is a difference between dealing with what you have to deal with and building a shrine to it.

When Lara was nearly two years old, O'Donnell had her propped on her hip and was getting ready to put a cracker into her mouth, like she'd done many times before. Lara—who had not shown awareness of any kind, had basically lived like the vegetable doctors told O'Donnell she would be—smiled at her mother, reached up to grab the cracker, and put it in her mouth. She made rapid improvement after that and grew up to become a lawyer and eventually work for the attorney general of Texas.

As Michele says now, "You have to keep your mind off of letting any reality become your identity."

The Method

> *"The eternal, blissful and natural state has been smothered by this life of ignorance."*
> — SRI RAMANA MAHARSHI, INDIAN GURU

In this experiment, you're going to pick an old story and you're going to flip it. You're going to take a reality that you have believed is absolute fact and you're going to actively look for its exact opposite.

I know you're thinking of something. If not, maybe some of these falsehoods that I used to repeat about myself (and have since rewritten, thank you very much) might give you some ideas:

- *I'm not that comfortable at parties.*
- *I've never been that great at relationships.*
- *I sometimes suffer from depression.*

It really doesn't matter. It simply has to be something you've repeatedly said and believed about yourself. Pick an identity that you've worn like a pair of your favorite jeans.

Okay, now you're going to rewrite it. And during this 72-hour time frame, you're going to look for evidence of this new reality. You're going to actively look for all signs—any fragment or pottery shard—of the opposite of this statement that, up until now, you have believed.

It Works Like the "Hi, Bob" Game

"Abandon your belief in deprivation."
— *A Course in Miracles*

When I was in college, "Hi, Bob" was a popular drinking game. Of course, in college, pretty much everything was an excuse for a drinking game.

This particular rendition was played in dorms, sorority houses, and college apartments all across America every night when *The Bob Newhart Show* came on. In case you haven't seen it, this popular sitcom from the late 1970s starred the deadpan comedian as psychiatrist Dr. Bob Hartley. A wide cast of patients walked in and out of his office and, of course, as people do, would say, "Hi, Bob!" Every time anyone—be it his wife, his secretary, or one of the many lovable characters that sought him out for counsel—said that all-important kicker, we participants loudly repeated it and took a big swig of our beers.

We couldn't wait to hear yet another "Hi, Bob!" We were on the edge of our seats, just like you're going to be while actively looking for evidence of the opposite of your long-held belief.

Lab Report Sheet

The Corollary: The Simon Cowell Corollary

The Theory: Nothing is absolute; only my thinking makes it so.

The Question: Is it possible that all the labels I've placed on myself, all the beliefs I've had about who I am, are nothing but a mirage that I've erroneously cemented in from years of believing in their veracity?

The Hypothesis: If I flip a long-held belief about myself, I will find just as much evidence in support of *that* reality.

Time Required: 72 hours

Today's Date: _____ **Time:** _____

Deadline for Receiving Answer: _____

The Approach: I will choose one of the many stories I've long believed about myself and I will spend three days investigating whether its opposite might be every bit as true.

Research Notes: _____

_____

_____

"Wake up expecting things."

— CHRISTINE BARANSKI, AMERICAN ACTRESS

RAINING CATS AND BLOGS

Lack Is a Mirage: The Three Best
Strategies for Getting to the Holy Land

"Avail yourself of possibilities."
— MIKE DOOLEY, AMERICAN AUTHOR

Peter Jackson was paid $20 million for the script of *King Kong*. You're not getting paid to create drama, so methinks it's time to write a different script. Here's how:

1. Give yourself an Academy Award for the amazing "drama" you've created thus far. In a world that brims with beauty and plenitude, the fact that you have been able to create such a convincing "story" of lack and struggle is truly an accomplishment. The special effects you have employed to overlook the world's unending largesse are truly mind-bending. Take a bow and ask yourself, "If I have been this successful at creating separation and pain (and believe me, we're all worthy of gold medals), then what else might I create with a little imagination?"

2. Use the feeling for rocket fuel. Once you get it that everything is your creation, you can use that intense feeling to propel you into a different story. The only reason you're still starring in the same, worn-out show (it should have been canceled in 1998 when *Seinfeld* went off the air) is because you've pitched a tent. You've completely forgotten that there are lots of other

destinations on the map. Because you endlessly harp about where you are and what's going wrong, you've driven in the stakes. At any time, you can move to a different location, a different story, a different reality.

3. Zip it up. You may not like the site of your present tent, but there is no need to tell the world about it. No matter where you're camped, there are blessings and miracles nearby. Instead of bellyaching about the script, the campsite, the life you're currently experiencing, focus in on everything that's going right. Once you begin to use your laser superpowers for possibilities, miracles, and joy, you will suddenly find yourself on a whole new stage, accepting a whole new Oscar.

EXPERIMENT #4

THE "I'M LOVING AND I KNOW IT" COROLLARY (*OR* THERE IS NO "THEM")

Meme: It's Me and You (and I'm Not So Sure about You) Against the World.

Worldview 2.0: Being in Love with Everyone and Everything Brings Me into Alignment with the FP.

> *"Everyone is God speaking.*
> *Why not be polite and listen . . . ?"*
> — Hafiz, translated by American poet Daniel Ladinsky

The Premise

In this experiment, you're going to prove that you actually love everyone (you just don't know it yet) and that anyone you're holding out of your heart is nothing but a hologram you created to showcase a part of yourself you've abandoned.

I can hear the boos now, see the banana peels waiting to be thrown.

"There is no way in hell," you're protesting, "that I love my boss. I'd be surprised if even his wife can stand him."

Or . . .

"I do *not* love my mother-in-law. She makes Osama Bin Laden look like a pussy cat."

As we move into Worldview 2.0, we're going to have to own up to the fact that anytime we're scared or in pain or sick or judging one of those holograms out there, we're not "in tune," so to speak, with the field of infinite potentiality. Because that's where all the magic happens, the sooner we can get on the same page as the FP, the sooner we can get this party started.

Our Source (the FP, God, whatever danged name you want to call it) loves everyone and everything. The FP, in fact, is like a teenage girl who thinks we're Justin Bieber. It loves us even when we dance with strippers, play naked beer pong, and crassly show off our wealth, something the teenybopper Beliebers have a hard time wrapping their minds around. Just like we can't wrap our minds around how much we are loved by Source. Source, in fact, sees us exactly as we are—giant, blissed-out balls of love—even when we're mean or judgmental or perceiving our mothers-in-law as Bin Laden clones. Which prompts me to point out: There's nothing inherently wrong with perceiving your mother-in-law as Bin Laden. But here's why you probably don't want to: When we see others (those holograms we think are separate people) as less than perfect, we move out of alignment with the field of infinite potentiality. We clog up the pipes of our own good.

Everything we "see" out there is produced by the projectors in our own minds. It's appealing to believe that your mean and nasty ole mother-in-law is out there, but she lives within your own consciousness. She's simply playing an essential part in your melodrama. You cast her in the play "out there" so you don't have to acknowledge the part of yourself that would take home the Oscar for best performance by an ogre.

The real joke's on the Bin Ladens of the world because they bought the ego's story. They invest ridiculous amounts of energy in Worldview 1.0's F--k My Life (FML) story. According to the FML story, our job is to identify a problem and then track down every single thing there is to know about it. Find out where it came from, find out why it's haunting us, and find out who's to blame. Heck, we might as well start a support group and a blog. We get so actively involved in eliminating a particular problem that it becomes our identity. But in "hating the problem" and investing our lives in eliminating it, we give it way more power than it actually has.

Tear Down Those Walls

"Something has got to hold it together. I'm saying my prayers to Elmer, the Greek god of glue."
— TOM ROBBINS, AMERICAN AUTHOR

If you've ever installed an ink-jet printer cartridge (and I know you have because they seem to need replacing every 50 or so pages), you've undoubtedly noticed the installation message on your computer screen, the one that asks you to match up the five or six horizontal lines. You're asked to pick which of these half dozen or so examples provides the very best alignment. The idea is that if the printer heads are properly aligned, you get clearer, crisper copy.

The same principle works in our daily lives. When we're properly aligned with the field of infinite potentiality, there's no resistance. There's nothing to keep the ink (or, in our case, the love and the joy) away. When the ink jets are properly aligned, everything flows smoothly, everything works.

Sadly, most of us spend much of our lives *out* of alignment. Instead of singing Louis Armstrong's "It's a Wonderful World," training ourselves for love and positive expectations, we slice and dice the apparent "what is."

Our reasoning goes like this:

- "Be nice to me. Then I'll think about loving you."

- "Quit dissing my political party. Then we can talk."

- "Show me the money. Then I'll feel joy."

But that's not how it works. That's not how you align with the FP.

You align with the FP by loving everyone, by seeing the "face of God" in everything, by feeling happy, by being joyful no matter what. Instead of letting the "apparent reality" dictate your feelings, you line up with the FP, which knows nothing but love, peace, and perfect contentment.

When you continue to bemoan the fact that so-and-so is not behaving, you deprive yourself of alignment. The FP is nothing but pure love, and when you're busy documenting and discussing "what appears to be," suffice it to say, you are *not* fully lined up. In fact, all these intentions you want to manifest? Once you line up with the FP, anything you could ever need or want shows up immediately. There's absolutely no resistance. In fact, *alignment* and *enlightenment,* a popular word in spiritual circles, are synonyms. Once you're aligned with the FP, you have everything. Everything.

So I repeat. The best way to line up your ink jets is to love every hologram. The apparent "what is" is old news. Ignore what doesn't please you. It's passé. It's history. And it will cease to be once you line up those love and joy ink jets.

One More Reason to Shout "Hallelujah!"

"Gratitude unlocks the fullness of life. It turns what we have into enough, and more. It turns denial into acceptance, chaos to order, confusion to clarity. It can turn a meal into a feast, a house into a home, a stranger into a friend."
— Melody Beattie, author of Codependent No More

It's pretty easy to be grateful when the sails of life are blowing your way. But what about the times when things "appear" not to be working out? My tack? Say "hallelujah!" anyway.

We, in our limited pea brains, don't always see the big picture. It's like standing with your nose against the pointillist painting. It looks like a bunch of dots. But when you step back and look again in gratitude, it becomes Georges Seurat's *A Sunday Afternoon on the Island of La Grande Jatte.*

Gail Lynne Goodwin, founder of InspiremeToday.com, told me a story that illustrates this perfectly. Not too long ago, she and a couple of friends had a girlfriends' outing planned. One of the friends, on the day of, woke up to find her daughter running a fever. She called Gail, whimpering about her bad luck. Gail responded in the way she responds to everything: "That's fabulous!"

"No, you didn't hear me," her girlfriend said. "I'm not going to be able to go today."

Again, Gail said, "That's fabulous!" She reminded her that she'd been needing some free time to sift through paperwork and that this so-called setback provided the perfect opportunity.

Her friend thanked Gail for the reminder, and not only did she end up having a delightful day with her daughter, but while cruising the Internet, she also came across the very house she'd been lusting after for three years. This dream house was way more than she felt she could afford, but on this day, while dealing with the disappointment of thwarted plans, she saw "her house" had gone into foreclosure and was selling for one-quarter of the initial price.

As Gail said, "She now has a contract on her dream home."

So, no matter what your judgments about your life may be, say, "Hallelujah!"

And be over-the-moon grateful that everything is working out for your good.

This Is the Best Thing to Ever Happen to Me

"The universe is wider than our views of it."

— HENRY DAVID THOREAU, AMERICAN PHILOSOPHER AND AUTHOR

Once you can say "This is the best thing to happen to me" about everything that happens in your life, you'll be aligned with the FP. Right now, most of us are heavily invested in the perception of issues and problems. The current dominant paradigm is built, brick by brick, with limitation, suffering, and pain.

But limitation, suffering, and pain are nothing but misinterpretations. It's like the perception is speaking Swahili and we're speaking English. The ultimate Truth is lost in the translation.

Here's just one example. Having your house flooded—not exactly a welcome addition to the old bucket list. But that's exactly what happened to a friend of mine who owns a house in Lyons, Colorado. During the summer of 2013, floods wiped out half the town, making big, national ain't-it-awful (AIA) headlines. But those AIAs turned the whole town upside down, bringing out the love that was always there, but masquerading as everyday reality.

Problems, pain, and disaster are often a Rosetta Stone for mastering the language of love. During regular reality (Worldview 1.0), we often don't hear the love. Our *Dancing with the Stars* judging minds are holding up number awful.

Who in their right mind would ask for a flood? Yet, that flood has reunited the community and brought love and generosity out into the open. My friend has been overwhelmed and moved by the giant balls of love in Lyons. Even though the flood knocked out her electricity, taking with it most creature comforts, she has everything that's important—a deep sense of belonging, appreciation for her community, and love out where it can be basked in. Over Thanksgiving, for example, students in the local high school baked pumpkin pies for everybody in town.

I posit that, on some level, we know exactly what we're doing and that we create these apparent "disasters" and "unloving people" to break through the walls we've erected. The love—the energy force—is always there, pulsing, throbbing, wanting to speak up, but often it takes a disaster like a flood for us to recognize it.

Everyone Is Your "Gayle King"

*"If the doors of perception were cleansed
every thing would appear to man as it is, infinite."*
— WILLIAM BLAKE, ENGLISH POET AND PRINTMAKER

Sean Penn, a brilliant actor, has played a wide range of roles over the years: he played a surfer stoner in *Fast Times at Ridgemont High,* almost single-handedly introducing the term *dude* into the American lexicon; a racist murderer in *Dead Man Walking;* a mentally handicapped father in *I Am Sam;* and gay-rights icon Harvey Milk, who was gunned down in the prime of his life, in *Milk.* In real life, none of us would choose any of these roles. They're unappealing and, on the surface anyway, difficult to live through.

Penn, of course, chose these roles because they helped him expand as an actor. They helped him grow. They helped him become hugely successful, winning an Academy Award and a Golden Globe for his Harvey Milk portrayal.

Similarly, I think that's why we often create holograms of unloving things—for the expansion it will create, for the "Academy Award" it will eventually reap in the big picture.

Our judging minds are so quick to leap to "OMG. That's a catastrophe." We shut down, start holding up the AIA cards. Become holier-than-thou.

Take sexual abuse, for example. Who in Worldview 1.0 could withhold judgment in such a situation, particularly when the abuse is perpetrated on a child? Yet, Louise Hay, who is virtually the Godmother to anybody who reads these kinds of books and whose life has blessed millions of people, probably wouldn't be the person she is today had she not gone through that particular AIA. Through this seeming AIA, she was able to find her own inner wisdom and realize the ball of love that she is.

Many things that at face value look like difficulties end up being miracles in disguise. The cancer that we might believe isn't fair can be a pathway to Truth. It can be a door to potent opportunities. We get to decide.

So instead of asking the question "Why do bad things happen to good people?" perhaps the better question is "Why do good people think bad things can even happen?" Bad is nothing but a judgment call, a judgment call we're not qualified to make. Just like *American Idol* hasn't requested your services next to JLo and Keith Urban, you aren't qualified to judge what is good and bad.

Once we wake up every morning and say, "This is the best thing to ever happen to me," we will move into alignment, where beauty and joy are free to rise. Then everyone becomes our best friend—our Gayle King.

I look forward to the day when we'll be able to recognize and call forth the love without creating the disaster. But until then, I, like Randy Jackson, am resigning from being a judge.

Anecdotal Evidence

"Relying on thought has been our escape route. The only instruction we need to follow from the mind is 'rest in presence.' This one instruction changes everything."
— SCOTT KILOBY, AUTHOR AND TEACHER

On April 15, 2013, two pressure-cooker bombs exploded near the finish line at the Boston Marathon. The world watched with horror as images of scarred and limbless people ran to safety.

James Costello was there at the finish line, rooting on a grade-school buddy, when the second bomb detonated right near his feet. Captured minutes later, a photograph of Costello, badly burned with his clothes in tatters, became one of the tragedy's iconic images. After two weeks and multiple surgeries at Massachusetts General Hospital, one involving pig grafts to replace his skin, Bim, as his friends call him, was transferred to Spaulding Rehabilitation Hospital in Boston, not something many of us would ever willingly choose.

But now, Costello says, "I'm actually glad I got blown up."

During his arduous rehab, he met Krista D'Agostino, a beautiful dark-haired nurse on temporary assignment at Spaulding, when she came to change his wound dressings. He invited her to a benefit for survivors of the Boston bombing and they've been dating ever since. And in December 2013, on a ten-day cruise through Europe, he proposed to her in Lyon, France.

"I wish nobody else had to have been blown up, but it ended up being the best thing that ever happened to me," says Costello, who to this day is still pulling metal shavings of bomb debris from his right leg. "I now realize why I was involved in the tragedy. It was to meet my best friend and the love of my life."

The Method

> *"In the practice of tolerance,*
> *one's enemy is the best teacher."*
>
> — DALAI LAMA, TIBETAN SPIRITUAL LEADER

If you thought Match.com or eHarmony was good at hook-ups, wait until you try this.

This experiment, which can be performed without an annoying monthly membership fee, is designed to prove two things: love isn't something you have to find (it's who you are); and when you're "in love" (with everything), you're aligned with Source, which makes all your intentions come flowing in.

Here's what I'd like you to do:

1. Be a love bomber. Get a pad of sticky notes (they come in all sorts of brilliant colors) and write love notes to the world. Stick them up everywhere. Tuck them into books at the library. Leave them on the backs of dollar bills. Tag posters on the subway.

2. Appreciate the world's most annoying person. I once heard spiritual author Wayne Dyer say that there's a photo of Rush Limbaugh, the conservative talk-show host, on his altar. It's there along with St. Francis, Lao-tzu, and other masters because loving Rush, who has been known to push a few buttons, offers us a Ph.D. program in loving unconditionally. So pick out someone who trips your triggers (I know you're thinking of someone) and begin looking for things to appreciate about him or her.

On a scale of 1 to 10, rate how you feel before performing these two acts and after.

Lab Report Sheet

The Corollary: The "I'm Loving and I Know It" Corollary

The Theory: There is no "them." It's only "us."

The Question: Is it possible that all people (and situations and events and other intolerable things) I can't stand are blessing me with opportunities to grow?

The Hypothesis: The more love I generate, the more I'll be in alignment with the field of infinite potentiality.

Time Required: 72 hours

The Approach: I will actively look for things to appreciate about "my enemy." I will try to see him or her in a different light. Maybe I can picture him as a young boy, being teased at school. Maybe I can appreciate her ferocity, however misguided it might seem. And then, after spending the next three days sending out love bombs to the world, I will gauge how I feel before and after.

How I feel before: _____

How I feel after: _____

Research Notes: _____

_____

_____

"Guard well our human chain."

— PETE SEEGER, AMERICAN FOLK SINGER AND ACTIVIST

RAINING CATS AND BLOGS

I Know Nothing

*"Incredible things happen all the time
when you buzz at the right level."*
— OVERHEARD AT STARBUCKS AND SHARED BY EITAN TOM AITCH

I've been thinking a lot about Hans Schultz. He is the fictional sergeant to Colonel Wilhelm Klink in the old TV series *Hogan's Heroes.*

Even though Schultz knew about the shenanigans of the Allied POWs who were running Special Operations from Stalag 13, he was famous for proclaiming to his inept colonel, "I know nothing" in a clipped, German accent.

I repeat that line (complete with the accent) quite often. In fact, it has become an important piece of my spiritual practice. I have learned that anytime I think I've figured something out, anytime I believe I've found the route to this intention or that dream, I promptly proceed to get in my own way. My understanding is sorely limited. But when "I know nothing," like Hans Schultz, I leave the gates wide-open for blessings to rush in.

For example, I got an incredible response to my first post on The Daily Love. It's a popular website run by Mastin Kipp, a young entrepreneur who recently appeared on Oprah's *Super Soul Sunday* as one of the Next Generation thought leaders. I happened to catch that episode, looked him up, and discovered that, lo and behold, he grew up in my hometown. I decided I wanted to write for The Daily Love, and I did everything I could think of to interest Mastin in my "brilliant wisdom." I even wrote an article about him in the local *Lawrence Magazine*. I mean, c'mon, we talked in person.

Those initial pitches? That initial scheme I came up with for getting on The Daily Love? Futile. Nada. Didn't work.

However, when I let go of my plan, repeated the Hans Schultz "I know nothing," and forgot all about it ("Set it and forget it" is a new mantra of mine), Madeline Giles, the former editor of The Daily Love—or the Love Curator, as she was known—contacted me. Out of the blue, she wrote to me, said she liked my new book, and wondered if I'd be up for contributing to The Daily Love.

So, Hans Schultz, thank you for proving that inspiration and important spiritual practices can come from anywhere.

EXPERIMENT #5

YOUR NEW B.F.F. COROLLARY (*OR* MONEY: IT'S NOT COMPLICATED)

Meme: Too Many to List Here.
See Bald-faced Lies Below.

Worldview 2.0: Money Is Nothing But
Energy and a Reflection of My Beliefs.

*"I discovered that making money was easy . . . [and] I
knew that this was not what I was here for."*
— PEACE PILGRIM, AMERICAN PACIFIST AND ACTIVIST

The Premise

This experiment will prove that money is nothing but energy and that it is only your baggage around money that keeps you from having it, enjoying it, and realizing that it is not what you are here for. Your current financial situation is a reflection of your beliefs and expectations. Once you change your beliefs and expectations, your entire financial situation will change.

Beliefs around money are completely skewed in World-view 1.0. We actually believe the big green is more important than our brothers and sisters. We put these strips of paper and metal coins (and now plastic cards etched with our names) on a pedestal and prostrate ourselves in undivided worship.

It's time to look these beliefs squarely in the eye and call them out as the big fat liars they are. Yes, these are the memes that were too lengthy to list.

Money, Money on the Wall

"If money was a person, in the way I felt about it, it would be practically like an unobtainable Hollywood movie star, or like some kind of God."
— GRACE BELL, TEACHER OF BYRON KATIE'S "THE WORK"

Most of us have an angst-ridden relationship with money. We think it's limited, demanding, and as unpredictable as Lindsay Lohan. We believe it's out of our control, and that forces higher than us pull the puppet strings. We have it tied up with jobs—jobs that, for the most part, we hate and resent. Thoughts like these, needless to say, do not for a happy relationship make.

Let's take an unflinching look at the top ten lies about money:

Big fat lie #1: You have to have it to be happy. People in developing countries, who are still in touch with the natural world (although the developed world is doing everything it can to erase this knowledge), laugh at the lengths to which we go to accumulate money and some of the ridiculous things it will buy. And on every single index of happiness, there is no relationship whatsoever to GDP.

Big fat lie #2: If you have it, you're happier. I have just two words to say: Owen Wilson. He's worth $60 million, and in 2007 he slit his wrists. Lucky for us, he wasn't successful, but he's proof positive that money cannot buy happiness. Another well-known actor, Jim Carrey, is famous for saying he wished everyone was rich (and famous) so they could see it's not the answer.

Big fat lie #3: You have to work your ass off to get it. Riddle me this: Who works harder—the eight-hour-a-day factory worker or Donald Trump? Some of the poorest people I know slave away at minimum-wage jobs, putting in more and more hours trying to get ahead. Money, at least in my life, often shows up unannounced. And all those e-mails I've been getting from *E-Squared* readers? There were countless stories from people who suddenly received unexpected money.

Big fat lie #4: There's only so much to go around. There's a $500 billion advertising machine whose sole job is to convince you that you are lacking and that there's only so much to go around. Once money and resources are defined as limited, every ounce of energy (what you say, what you think, what you do) revolves around overcoming this lack and protecting what you already have.

Big fat lie #5: More of it is better. A natural dance partner to "there's only so much to go around," this big fat lie distances us from enjoying what we already have. When we're constantly focused on the next big thing, worrying that we need more, more, more to avoid being left out, we don't experience joy with what's already right in front of us. Excess money often creates entitlement and isolation that diminishes the wealth of human connection. I have often argued that amassing seven billion, the dollar amount Donald Trump claims to be worth, is not that different from hoarding old newspapers, leaky buckets, and all the other junk collecting in the homes of the dysfunctional folks we watch on the A&E show *Hoarders*.

Big fat lie #6: The economic system is set in stone; there's nothing we can do to change it. Even though it often seems unfair (the rich keep getting richer, and those with the most money wield all the power), we continue to play the game, continue to buy the big fat lie that it's "just the way it is." That there's nothing we can do about it. These assumptions, traditions, and habits not only trap us into resignation, but they also block a more accurate vision that prosperity is possible for all. As far back as the 1970s, the great futurist and humanist Buckminster Fuller recognized that human civilization had reached a turning point where a new paradigm was possible, a paradigm in which all of us could have enough food, water, housing, and land to lead fulfilling and productive lives.

Big fat lie #7: Money is bad, and people who have a lot of it are really bad. Remember that money-and-camels thing from the Bible? I don't know whether that was the genesis of the rumor or not, but I do know there's nothing inherently wrong with money. Money is a shadow of something much deeper. As Kate Northrup teaches in her book, *Money: A Love Story,* a more productive way to think about money is to see it as an exchange of value for value. Or, as my new friend Felicia Spahr says, "Money is everyone's B.F.F. and they don't even know it."

Big fat lie #8: Jobs blow. Work is one of those things we have tied to the railroad track with unhappiness. When it comes to our jobs, every neural pathway in our bodies screams "let me out of here." We believe it's the weekends and the vacations we want and that work is only a means to an end. As long as we associate these two together, we miss out on massive amounts of fun and joy.

Big fat lie #9: The only way to get it is to have a job. Money and work go together like pancakes and syrup, like Russia and vodka, like celebrities and paparazzi. Although money and jobs have certainly been dating for quite some time, they're far from married. Or certainly shouldn't be for people who want to live an abundant life. I haven't had a job in 20-some years.

Big fat lie #10: It's a distant, magical demigod. As you're starting to realize, the list of big fat money lies could fill the Grand Canyon. So in the interest of getting to the good stuff, the *truth* about the world and its largesse, I'm lumping a few more into this lie (*I'm different from people who have money; To get it you have to cheat and lie; If you make it, there's no time for play;* and *There's no possibility of getting things without money*) and calling it good.

So that's pretty much money in Worldview 1.0. Ready to look at Money 2.0?

Untangling the Money Morass

"There is a natural law of abundance which pervades the entire universe, but it will not flow through a doorway of belief in lack and limitation."
— PAUL ZAITER, ABUNDANCE TEACHER

Remember those beliefs and expectations that play out in our financial lives? They need to be changed. Abundance consciousness, which is what creates money in the first place, is equally available to everyone. Like air, it's free . . . and anyone who wants can develop it. The simple fact of being human guarantees you have more abundance potential than you could possibly experience in a lifetime. And once you attain abundance consciousness, money will follow you around, chase you down, and spit in your face.

But first you have to get these six things, these paradigms from Worldview 2.0:

1. Money isn't real. It's a form of exchange. And all material things have no value except a random number we assign to them. That number can change at any time. A house that's worth $500,000 today might sell for twice that tomorrow. Money-market funds have been known to grow by 25 percent in one week. None of it is real except the value we give it.

Money, or what we think of as money—bills and coins—is merely a tool that demonstrates a person's wealth consciousness. And according to prosperity teacher David Cameron Gikandi, only 4 percent of money in banks (depending on the country) exists in physical form.

Money is always a shadow of something else. And how it plays out in your life revolves around two things: the value you place upon yourself and the ingredients you've placed in your money expectation beaker.

2. Money is an energy that forms around your thoughts. I once interviewed a woman who gave all her money away. Actually, I've interviewed several people who gave their fortunes away. Millionaires sloughing off riches is a hugely popular topic at *People* magazine. This particular person came from money. Her grandfather was some famous industrialist. Her parents owned houses all over the world. She didn't feel right having such excess when others went hungry, so she gave away her sizable inheritance, the whole dang shooting match. And she began giving workshops on contributing to the greater good. Before she knew it, she'd amassed another million.

Moral of the story? You can take the money out of the girl's wealth consciousness, but you can't take the wealth consciousness out of the girl.

3. The world seen clearly without the lens of lack and limitation is wildly abundant. Bernard Lietaer, former senior officer of the Belgian Central Bank and chief architect of the euro currency, says in his book *Of Human Wealth* that the idea of scarcity is nothing but misguided cultural programming. In other words, a meme that has spread across the globe. Even though we consider scarcity and the greed it provokes to be a normal, legitimate reality, neither exists in nature. Not even in human nature.

Examine your body, that body that's continually harping about lack and limitation. It has more than 50 trillion cells. Do you have any idea how many 50 trillion is?

Your eyes, those eyes that choose to focus so much attention on a tiny four-inch screen, have 100 million receptors,

100 million you could use to enjoy a rising moon, the Big Dipper, four-leaf clovers.

4. There is no shortage of anything. I remember picking grapes at a vineyard one fall. The owners of this vineyard, in a move rivaling Tom Sawyer's fence-painting scheme, invite locals out to the fields for the opportunity to harvest their grapes. It's so popular that there's a waiting list every year. Yes, people elbow each other out of the way for the chance to perform a task that the owners, before hatching this genius strategy, once paid migrant workers to do.

I am so grateful that I participated because it showed me in living color just how bountiful the world really is. There were so many grapes that we couldn't even get them all. Many had fallen to the ground before we arrived with our baskets. There was no way anybody could be there and not recognize the pressed-down and running-over reality.

Abundance is forever on display in the natural world. Just look at a tree. It has thousands of individual leaves, and as for the number of trees on this planet? I couldn't hazard a guess. Or try counting the blades of grass in one square foot of your front yard. Mother Nature (aka the natural world before humans imposed fear on her) provides for every single need.

5. Everything you *really* need is already provided. You are fine right now whether you have money or not. Although we tend to pair money with such desirables as security, ease, relaxation, approval, and joy, we can have every one of these things without piles of money in our account. All of them are included in our inheritance. They're given to us completely free of charge. Sadly, we barely recognize them behind the Halloween mask of the big fat lies from the previous section.

Here are a few of your other prized possessions, or they would be if you weren't so busy thinking lack. Did you have to make the sun come up this morning? Say thank you! Do you have to order your heart to pump blood through your body, 36 million beats per year? Do you have to schedule your lungs to draw in fresh, clear oxygen?

If we focus on the planet's unending largesse, rather than on the marketers' drumbeat of limitation, on the bounteous gifts that spread out before us on every side rather than on TV commercials that suggest erectile dysfunction, depression, and sleeping problems, then we can rewrite the dominant paradigm.

6. It is only our illusory belief in limitation that keeps our riches away. The only real difference between me and, say, Donald Trump is that I choose not to carry my riches around. It's comforting to know that anything I could ever want is available to me, but why flaunt it or drag around a bunch of material baggage?

No, my role model is Peace Pilgrim, who, when she was very young, made an important discovery: "Making money is easy." Which is why she could give up her earthly possessions and walk around the world with nothing but the clothes on her back. As she said about her 28-year journey, "Life is full and life is good. . . . There is a feeling of always being surrounded by all of the good things, like love and peace and joy. It seems like a protective surrounding."

That's all anyone really needs. To know with sure conviction that the world is limitless, abundant, and strangely accommodating.

Anecdotal Evidence

"I strongly encourage you to let go of these beliefs.
They are inaccurate and melodramatic
and they do not serve you."

— CHERYL STRAYED, AMERICAN AUTHOR

Like everyone else on the planet, I received my engraved invitation to participate in the 2008 recession. Normally, I send regrets to those kinds of offers.

I learned ages ago that opportunities for pain and suffering are always going to be available and that if I was going to live with intention, it's best to steer clear. I'd have never become the author of 17 books, a reporter for *People* magazine, and a world traveler if I'd accepted the onslaught of "negative invitations."

"That's not possible," naysayers insisted on telling me. "It's hard to write a book. Even harder to sell it. You're an unknown from Kansas. You got B's in your journalism classes, for God's sake."

"Talk to the hand," I'd always say to those voices. "That may be your way of seeing things, but I choose a different reality, a higher path."

But after three years of ever-increasing income, even being in a position to turn down a fourth project for *National Geographic,* I took the ego's bait. By then, a constant stream of bad news dominated the headlines. My profession, journalism and book publishing, was among the hardest hit by the global downturn. Publishers were cutting back their lines, lowering their advances. Many of my colleagues in the newspaper business were suddenly without work.

Again, I normally don't listen to such nonsense. I much prefer a spiritual reality that proclaims abundance no matter what the circumstances. But by 2009, after little by little letting the dire news seep in, I plucked the aforementioned recession invitation out of the trash. I decided to take just a peek.

The party was in full swing. My agent was repeating the "nothing's selling" mantra over by the punch bowl. Regular clients were on the corner sofas, moaning about the economy and their need to buy less.

Before I knew what happened, I bunny hopped right into the middle of the celebration. I began singing the "ain't it awful" blues along with the party's deejay. I told anybody who'd listen about my hard times. Before long, I convinced everyone I know that my career as an independent author was over. I even fooled them into believing that, after all these years on my own, I was old, washed-up, and as yesterday as the History Channel.

I actually reveled in the sympathy.

Then one day, I got out my beat-up copy of *Think and Grow Rich*. As I read Napoleon Hill's words about thoughts being "things," I suddenly got it. Look how powerful my thoughts and words had been. Look what I'd done to myself. If I could create this disaster with nothing but my thoughts, then I could just as easily create the opposite.

When I think back about it now, I'm slightly embarrassed. How could I have fallen so bumpily off the wagon I'd used so successfully for so many years? I know good and well how this stuff works. I know that I create my own reality. I know that listening to doomsayers is the most futile exercise in the world.

I wasted no time using Hill's famous advice. Within a week, I had two new assignments. The book contract for *E-Squared* came next. Rather than live frugally, the advice my friends were freely passing out, I decided to spend the summer overseas, volunteering and letting my newly recovered faith pay the bills.

That decision to affirm "I am prosperous, and of course I can afford to travel overseas to volunteer" was the beginning of a more fruitful life.

Needless to say, I've taken that beautifully engraved invitation and ripped it to shreds. And don't bother sending any more. Because from now on, my RSVPs to any negativity will say one thing: "Have a good time. But don't expect to find me there."

The Method

> *"If you can see it in your mind,*
> *you can hold it in your hand."*
> — BOB PROCTOR, AUTHOR OF *YOU WERE BORN RICH*

Because money is so fraught with fear and antiquated old paradigms, I'm posing two sub-hypotheses (like I said, the world—and this chapter—is wildly abundant) in this experiment to prove the main hypothesis: *If I change my beliefs about money, my financial situation will change.*

Each of the two experiments takes three days.

Experiment #1:
Johnny Moneyseed (*or* The Circle Can't Be Broken)

> *"You don't have to 'create' financial*
> *abundance. It's already there."*
> — BOB SCHEINFELD, AUTHOR OF *BUSTING LOOSE FROM THE MONEY GAME*

The sub-hypothesis: If I give away money, I will receive even more money.

It's an inalterable principle. "What you give comes back to you multiplied and running over."

During the three days of this experiment, you are going to seed money. You're going to leave small bills (or large ones if that's more to your liking) with notes about your newfound beliefs about the nature of abundance. You're going to do this freely, playfully, and openly.

My daughter Taz and I did this recently in Chicago. I was writing a travel story about the mighty Peninsula. If it's not ringing any bells, let me just say that this is where all the A-listers stayed when they came to Chicago to bid Oprah adieu. We could see the Magnificent Mile from our suite. We shopped, saw *The Book of Mormon*, and, of course, made a return engagement to Second City. In the audience, not on the stage.

We also performed the secret mission I'm asking you to perform. We took a stack of $5 bills and left them at bus stops, taped to park benches. We pinned them into clothes at the stores on Magnificent Mile. With each fiver, we left an anonymous note about the abundance of the universe and how this is just one small sign of how much whoever finds it is loved.

I know $5 isn't much (one of these days, we plan to leave hundies), but for us it's about "being" who we want to be—confident, freely giving—and knowing that as we give, so shall we receive.

We were doing what you'll be doing in this experiment—building muscle, practicing "being" what you want to be—united with all that is, knowing with complete surety you are provided for in every way.

Record what comes back to you during the 72 hours.

As for me, *E-Squared* surged to #1 on the *New York Times* bestseller list within a few weeks of that experiment.

Experiment #2:
Pennies from Heaven

*"Poverty consciousness results from
wearing . . . blinders to the abundance of life."*
— GLENDA GREEN, AMERICAN PAINTER AND AUTHOR

The sub-hypothesis: Money is easy to come by.

I learned this experiment from Greg Kuhn, my buddy and fellow author who writes about the same stuff I do. He has penned a whole series of books about applying quantum physics to the law of attraction. (Check out his website, www.whyquantumphysicists.com, and his acclaimed *Why Quantum Physicists . . .* series.) I particularly love the game he invented called "Grow a Greater Greg," only when I play it, I change the title to "Grow a Greater Pam." Doesn't have quite the same ring, but you get the point.

Greg gave me permission to share this experiment that, as he says, puts you into an abundance mind-set and forms coherence between the quantum field and your financial abundance.

It's pretty simple. For the next three days, intend to find pennies:

- On the ground
- In your pockets
- In your car
- On the sidewalk
- Everywhere

Conjure them by dwelling not on *Where are they?* but on *How exciting it is to manifest a penny!* After all, how challenging

144

is it to find a penny? Pennies are the fruitcake of the currency world. Some people throw them away because they consider them worthless.

And, if you want to look at it that way, pennies *are* sort of worthless. So you'll have no trouble manifesting them every day, because they are simply no big deal.

The Quantum Field Doesn't Care If You Play Tricks on It

But here's where the experiment kicks in. You're actually going to trick the quantum field. Don't worry—the quantum field won't care; it makes no judgments, it just responds.

After finding a penny, privately celebrate it like you just won the lottery. Go way overboard. Way over the top. Get silly with it. Privately shout hosannas to the universe!

Doesn't sound realistic to celebrate a "dumb" little old penny? After all, a penny certainly does not represent the abundance you *truly* desire, does it?

But here's how you trick the quantum field with this game. What you celebrate is *not* the amount the penny represents; you celebrate the principle it represents. You celebrate the principle that the universe is infinitely abundant and that manifesting is child's play.

You are celebrating the universe "goosing" you with this penny—getting your attention and saying, "Hey, my wonderful, most special child! I am at your service, and I can and will create anything your heart desires! And I can create your heart's desire just as easily as I created this penny! Isn't that awesome?!"

145

The Quantum Field Wants
to Give You More of What You Celebrate

And the trick is, the quantum field doesn't know the difference between your celebrating the amount versus celebrating the reminder. The quantum field simply forms coherence with your energy of "this is awesome" and readily lines up to bring you more of it.

And you benefit because you can truly, realistically, and believably celebrate the *reminder of abundance* each penny represents in the super-grand, Fourth-of-July-fireworks style I'm suggesting.

Lab Report Sheet

The Corollary: Your New B.F.F. Corollary

The Theory: Money is nothing but energy and a reflection of my beliefs.

The Question: Am I blocking abundance by hanging on to a bunch of old ideas that no longer serve me?

The Hypothesis: If I change my beliefs about money, the world's natural abundance will rush in.

> *Sub-hypothesis #1:* If I give away money, I will receive even more money.

> *Sub-hypothesis #2:* Money is easy to come by.

Time Required: 72 hours each

Date of First Experiment: _____ **Time:** _____

Deadline: _____

Results: _____

Date of Second Experiment: _____ **Time:** _____

Deadline: _____

Results: _____

The Approach: I'm going to put on my acting heels and act like the diva I was meant to be. I'm going to observe how the universe responds. For the first 72 hours, I'm going to give what I want to get, trusting that it is impossible to outgive the universe. And for the final 72 hours, I'm going to align with the quantum field by hunting for pennies.

Research Notes: _____

_____

_____

"I realized that I needed to do a little remixing on how I felt about money."

— FELICIA SPAHR, AUTHOR OF *SELLING FOR SUCCESS*

RAINING CATS AND BLOGS

Monetize, Schmonetize:
The Real Juice Is in the Gift Economy

*"When you realize there is nothing lacking,
the whole world belongs to you."*
— LAO-TZU, CHINESE PHILOSOPHER AND POET

You don't need Alex Trebek or "buzzwords for $5,000" to know that the Internet's top trend right now is "How do I monetize my website? My blog? My Twitter feed?" Even YouTube offers monetization to prolific video uploaders.

Since I've been accused of being a "subversive presence on the planet," I want to talk about the exact opposite.

How do you un-monetize your life? How do you go against the culture's dominant paradigm of wanting to "always get, get, get" and practice what's known as the gift economy?

The gift economy, a philosophy more than a financial practice, is one in which people refuse to believe in scarcity and fear. Instead of always trying to "get more," a gift economy is for those looking for ways they can give. It's so radical that most people can't even understand it.

I pitched a story about the gift economy to my editor at *People* magazine. She loves heroes, good news, and heartwarming human-interest stories. But even though I gave her three specific examples of people working solely in the gift economy, she couldn't understand it. "But how does it work?" she kept repeating.

It works, although I could never explain this spiritual belief to her, because once you give up your incessant fear and belief that it's a dog-eat-dog, every-man-for-himself world, abundance can't help but show up in your life. It's actually the reality of the human condition, but as long as we're "monetizing" and erecting walls of fear, we block abundance.

Perhaps the best example of the gift economy is Nipun Mehta, the guy I begged my *People* editor to let me profile. In April 1999, when he was 25, he gave up his lucrative paycheck at Sun Microsystems to become a full-time volunteer. A fan of Gandhi, who said, "Be the change you wish to see in the world," Mehta started "giving" as an experiment. He started with money (he gave to charity), moved on to giving of his time (volunteering at a hospice), and then decided he'd go full-time, giving of himself unconditionally with no strings attached. Thirteen years later, his experiment has been a huge success.

He started a free restaurant and a free inspirational magazine and has given away hundreds of millions of dollars in free tech services. He's a Stanford-trained engineer who was raking it in during the dot-com heyday. But he wasn't sure that's where happiness lay. He works with a network of more than 100,000 volunteers who operate on three principles:

1. Everything is strictly volunteer. Money is *never* charged.

2. No one ever *asks* for money. Many charities do good work, but they all ask for donations. They

do endless fund-raising. He says that forces people into a needy space and he prefers coming from a belief in abundance and the goodness of humankind. And indeed, money has shown up in spades (from the billionaire founder of Sony, as just one example) and from anonymous donors who send in checks for $10,000 or more. But Mehta and crew *never* ask or expect.

3. They focus on small actions. "You just take care of what you can touch, give to whatever is in front of you," he says, and the ripple effects have organized into what he calls their own magic. "I can tell you story after story."

The Karma Kitchen that he and fellow volunteers started in Berkeley, California (there are no prices on the menu and the check reads $0.00), spawned Karma Kitchens in Washington, D.C., and Chicago.

"We don't charge for anything, nor do we advertise anything. The project is sustained by anonymous friends who donate what they can, not as a payment for what they have received but as a pay-it-forward act for someone they don't know," Mehta says.

In place of financial capital, Mehta and his network of volunteers are building social capital, synergy capital, and a type of subtle capital beyond definition.

Another one of my heroes is Ethan Hughes, who started the Superheroes Alliance, a group of 700 living, breathing superheroes. He and his wife, Sarah, give away everything they grow on their farm at the Possibility Alliance. They've given away goats, fruit bushes, seeds, soil, and compost. They've donated trees to every major city in Missouri. Most important, they host more than 1,500 people a year who come to their farm from around the country to learn about permaculture. Permaculture classes normally start at about $1,500, but Ethan and Sarah give them away free.

"At first people are shocked," Ethan explains. "So few mainstream Americans believe someone would actually give something away for free with no ulterior motives. We're in a cynical society that rarely trusts someone who says, 'Hey, I just want to help.'"

The Hugheses and their network of volunteers have helped build a library, bucked hay for a fellow farmer, cleaned up city parks, and donated something like 50,000 hours of community service . . . all with no expectation.

"It's really important to me to create access, and the gift economy is about access," Ethan says. "It's about sharing an experience of generosity that has the potential to shift both the giver and the recipient."

That's why I say, "Forget monetizing." Think about something important, like the gifts you have to give.

EXPERIMENT #6

THE NATURE VS. NEWS COROLLARY (*OR* WHY YOU SHOULD REALLY GET OUT MORE)

Meme: My Job Is to Rule, Control, and Protect Myself from Nature.

Worldview 2.0: The Field of Infinite Potentiality Offers a Divine 24-7 Buzz.

"The earth has music for those who listen."
— GEORGE SANTAYANA, AMERICAN PHILOSOPHER AND POET

The Premise

Quick. Tell me which phase the moon is in? Today, right now. Is it waxing? Waning? Is it full? Is it new?

What? You have no idea?

Yet, I bet you know exactly which new dysfunction happened today in Congress, which new terror threat it's now necessary to fear. You might have even posted a warning on Facebook (and felt noble for doing so) about tainted dog food or about some new strain of bacteria recently discovered in restaurant salad bars.

What I'd like to suggest in this three-day experiment is that all the important stuff you need to know is happening right outside your window, right there in your neighborhood, right in your own heart. And that what you pick up from the news media has no real relevance to your life. Except for the blocks it erects between you and the FP.

I realize this is probably a striking departure. From the time your third-grade teacher instructed you to bring in a news clipping from the local paper, you've been taught that "news" is absolute fact, vitally important to your well-being and something that really sharp and together people follow with zealous abandon. After all, it adds to your swagger to be able to talk current events at parties, to be able to whip out your command of the latest headlines on job interviews.

This experiment will prove that "news" is just one corporation's opinion, more or less irrelevant to your well-being, and that *really* sharp and together people couldn't care less what newscasters are blathering on about today. The people I admire and hope to emulate know the only thing that really matters is the indestructible joy and pulse of life being broadcast from every tree, every star, every bird on the planet. They know that real life (as opposed to the material stuff the news media places on a vaunted pedestal) is created from being in tune with the universal broadcast, the Sacred Buzz.

This experiment will prove that the media, that nameless group of outlets that dictate reality, have it all wrong. And that the most important thing you could ever do for yourself is pay attention to the collective rhythm and wisdom emanating from the larger whole. By synchronizing yourself with nature's biorhythms, you'll tap into a whole new vein of consciousness. You'll connect with a sentient universe pervaded by an always-vibrating divine buzz. I know it sounds big and cosmic and perhaps even beyond your ken, but it's really the most natural thing in the world and, once you get the hang of it, a gazillion times more resourceful and richer in content than anything Bill O'Reilly might say.

By entering into reverent communion with the natural world (and, yes, that's the world right outside your window, no need to plan another eco-vacation), you'll be led on wild adventures into magical and invisible realms.

The Throbbing, Pulsing Now

"Even though the truth is absolutely out there, it's not necessarily what people pay attention to."
— Ev Williams, co-founder of Twitter

This experiment will show you that real wisdom is readily available when you turn off the bombardment of sensation known as the news. By investing in the fake news, the made-up news, the crap we read on the Internet, we miss the truly relevant news that's happening right here. Right now. What is happening on the set of Jennifer Aniston's latest flick or what John Boehner did or didn't say has no real relevance to your life.

Ignoring and discounting things like the stars, the plants, and the sliver of a waxing moon, whose cycles affect everything from tides to fiddler crabs to our sleep habits, blinds us to a major force of energy that we could and should be using in our favor. Being disconnected from the natural world wreaks havoc on our bodies. Ignoring things that affect us deeply and slavishly following things that have little or no impact causes stress, depression, and anxiety.

If we want to create more energy and therefore more "bandwidth" for a joyful life, we must begin to pay attention to things that matter. And let go of all the things that don't.

True Confession

"Media. I think I have heard of her.
Isn't she the one who killed her children?"
— NEIL GAIMAN, BRITISH AUTHOR

I might as well just say it.

I, Pam Grout, am a member of the world's largest terrorist organization.

As a freelance journalist who writes for *People* magazine, CNN, *The Huffington Post,* and other media outlets, I plead guilty, here and now, for having perpetuated rumors, exaggerations, and untruths. In other words, promoting terror.

One of the first tenets I learned in the hallowed halls of Kedzie at Kansas State University, where I attended journalism school, was "If it bleeds, it leads." That wouldn't be a problem if we didn't form so many of our opinions from the almighty news media. But we actually buy the crazy headlines. We actually believe this stuff.

Recently, one of the top trending stories on *Huffington Post* was about the dangers of pathogenic microbes on restaurant lemon wedges. Even though these microbes are ubiquitous (the researcher also found them on ketchup bottles, salt and pepper shakers, menus, and table surfaces), the headline that convinced hundreds of thousands to gasp in fear and quickly click to the link was this: "This Will Make You Never, Ever Want to Put a Lemon Wedge In Your Water Again."

I mean, how can you resist a headline like that?

Which is what the news is all about. Coming up with a sound bite or a news peg that will scare viewers or readers into paying attention, giving them a click or a like, making their numbers look good so advertisers will buy more ads.

Again, putting our faith in this nonsense wouldn't be an issue if our thoughts and their resulting beliefs and consciousness weren't such powerhouses. But our consciousness and our thoughts are musclemen, stepping out into the field of potentiality and bringing back the very circumstances, weather, disease, and dysfunction we invest in. Because we form so many of our opinions from the almighty news media, we should all be high-fiving and fist-bumping each other for the mere fact that we haven't put a razor blade to our wrists yet.

But here's what I know. What we see in the news media is a tiny speck of a reality far removed from true Reality. It's so limited in dimension and scope of understanding that to pay such close attention is like unknowingly having one of those "please kick me" signs pinned to your back. Combined with the lessons we learned from our parents (*Money doesn't grow on trees . . . It's important to grow up, work hard, and put your nose to the grindstone . . . Johnny, don't you dare go outside this house without your pants on . . .*) and our own resulting terrorist thoughts, we're pretty much screwed.

Except we aren't.

Mass media show the blood, the ambulances, the crying family members. But in my work as a reporter for *People* magazine, where, yes, I report on tornadoes and kidnappings and whole towns being washed away by floods, I witness the most incredible displays of generosity, the very finest of the human spirit.

It's Alive!

"It is only human arrogance, and the fact that the lives of plants unfold in what amounts to a much slower dimension of time, that keep us from appreciating their intelligence and consequent success."

— MICHAEL POLLAN, AMERICAN AUTHOR

In this experiment, you're going to tune out the news and tune in nature's Divine Broadcast that forever proclaims its love. This Sacred Buzz can be heard in every crocus poking through the ground. In every mockingbird ditty. In every cool breeze caressing your cheek.

For the next three days, you're going to cast your line into the collective knowledge of the universe. You're going to commune with nature, get intimate with the natural world. You're going to take time to listen to the planet and all her creatures, who, despite our constant harassment, still understand balance and the divine equilibrium.

According to those who have taken time to listen, nature imparts volumes of information. Of course, you do have to lay aside a lot of preconceived notions, dogmas, and personal prejudices.

Luther Burbank—the famous botanist who identified more than 800 new plant species, including the Shasta daisy, the freestone peach, and the russet potato—believed that getting in harmony with the universe was the only worthy source of "news." Tuning in to the glowing, luminous natural world was how he successfully crossbred the hundreds of new species that he advertised in his wildly successful catalog, *New Creations in Fruits and Flowers*. He believed all of us can receive messages from the magnetic, electrical, and vibrational forces of the universe.

More recently, Michael Pollan, in an article for *The New Yorker*, reported on a new breed of plant scientists who are proving that there's a lot more operating here in the universe than we initially believed and that what we can't see with the naked eye is more important than what we do see.

They Lock People Up for This

"We were meant to be
the only players on this stage."
— DANIEL QUINN, AUTHOR OF *ISHMAEL*

Yes, in this experiment we're going to play around with a little interspecies communication. You're going to talk to a tree. Or a plant or something that you have always believed was incapable of talking back. Don't laugh. Michael Crichton, the Harvard-educated doctor who left medicine to write books and movie screenplays (*Jurassic Park*), as well as create TV shows (*ER*), spent a couple of weeks in the California desert talking to a cactus. In his memoir, *Travels,* he wrote about a phone-free, drug-free workshop with Joy Brugh, also a doctor, where he learned to meditate, see and move energy, and yes, get guidance from a cactus.

As he explained, he was skeptical and not really sure he wanted to admit to talking to a battered phallic cactus with thorns and scars. Or let on that he broke down sobbing when, on the last day, the cactus said to him, "It's been good having you here with me." Even after he returned home, he questioned his sanity, wondered if he'd made any significant personal gains.

"The energy work was real. The meditations were real, but what good was it if you couldn't apply it to your daily life?" he asked.

It wasn't until later when he looked back and saw that, within eight months of returning from the desert, he had changed his relationships, his residence, his work, his diet, his interests, and his goals.

"In fact," he said, "I changed everything in my life that could be changed. These changes were so sweeping that I couldn't see what was happening while I was in the midst of them."

And there was one other change, too.

"I've become very fond of cacti, and I always have some around, wherever I live."

Anecdotal Evidence

"You already have inside you everything you've ever wanted or looked for elsewhere."

— SARA AVANT STOVER, AUTHOR OF THE WAY OF THE HAPPY WOMAN

George Washington Carver—the great American scientist and inventor who came up with hundreds of uses for the lowly legume and practically saved the economy of the South after the boll weevil devastated the cotton crop—knew all about the Divine Broadcast. Not only was he one of the first Americans to be inducted into Britain's Royal Society of Arts, but he was also friends with three American Presidents.

And while, yes, he had several advanced degrees and taught at several colleges, he was the first to admit that all his "scientific" discoveries, the brilliance that made him so famous, came from his connection to God or what I call the field of potentiality (FP). Every morning, very early, Carver walked for many miles. He connected with nature, and it was that communion, indeed the plants themselves, that told him how to turn peanuts and soybeans and sweet potatoes into the more than 100 commercial products he developed.

As he said, "I think of nature as an unlimited broadcasting station, through which God speaks to us every hour, if we will only tune in. . . . Reading about nature is fine, but if a person walks in the woods and listens carefully, he can learn more than what is in books."

Carver said he never had to grope for methods. Anything he needed to know was easily revealed to him. "Without God to draw aside the curtain," he said, "I would be helpless."

Likewise, Albert Einstein, the man we credit as being the world's foremost genius, was connected to this higher energy.

Call it what you will, but nature/God/the FP has answers to every alleged "problem" and "devastated economy" that seems to challenge us. Once we let go of all we think we "know" and make it our goal to connect to this unlimited, all-knowing, all-loving force, new discoveries and brilliance will rush in from every side.

Becoming a Horse (or Plant or Tree) Whisperer

"Anything will give up its secrets if you love it enough."
— George Washington Carver, American scientist

So yeah, I'm about to suggest that you engage in what most people would label "crazy behavior."

Dr. Doolittle aside, most civilized Westerners don't partake of riveting conversation with their ferrets. Yet, the animal world, the plant world, the world that we discount with our emphasis on a five-senses reality, has a lot to say.

Many aboriginal people consider the ability to send and receive messages, to communicate and talk with all of nature, no big deal. It isn't a special gift. It's a part of everyday life, as natural and normal as using vocalized language. People who can't access the "hum of the universe" seem like an anomaly to them, the way we view someone born deaf.

Psychologist Robert Wolff, who spent several decades working with the Sng'oi of the Malaysian rain forest, says it used to mystify him when his friend Ahmeed, without the use of telephones, clocks, or calendars, would somehow know the exact day he was returning from the West and would be there at the drop-off waiting to help with his bags. In stark contrast to today's industrial societies, the Sng'oi possessed an acute and uncanny attunement to the energies and emotions of their surroundings, giving them what Wolff called "superhuman" powers of knowing.

Intrigued by the tribe's complete lack of fear and anxiety, Wolff eventually apprenticed himself to Ahmeed, eventually learned to still his verbal, analytical mind and experience what he calls the "unity of all life." He said the Sng'oi were in touch with that deep connection that the rest of us keep trying to regain through books, tapes, and seminars. Although the Sng'oi and their rain forest were eventually cleared by Komatsu bulldozers, Wolff, in this book *Original Wisdom*, says this trusting, intuitive connection, this original intelligence, can be reclaimed.

According to Anna Breytenbach, a former Silicon Valley IT professional who now works with veterinarians and conservation officials as an animal communicator, the ability to transfer information between minds, be it human or animal, is hardwired into the design of our brains. The trick, she says, is becoming empathetically connected and opening up to the electromagnetic impulses generated by thoughts and emotions.

No Struggle When You're One with Nature

*"It takes a touch of genius—and a lot of
courage—to move in the opposite direction."*
— ALBERT EINSTEIN, GERMAN-BORN PHYSICIST

On December 14, 2005, the *San Francisco Chronicle* ran a story about a female humpback whale, who, after being freed from a spiderweb of crab traps and lines, went back to thank the divers who spent several hours untangling her. After swimming in joyous circles, she went back to each diver and, one at a time, nudged them and looked them in the eye, a profound experience that one of the divers said "changed" him forever.

I also love this story about a herd of African elephants who came to salute their former trainer after his death. Even though he had retired and hadn't worked with them in several years, they somehow knew he had died, and walked many miles to form a circle of respect around his home.

The Method

*"All I know is what I read in the papers,
and that's an alibi for my ignorance."*
— WILL ROGERS, AMERICAN HUMORIST

For the next three days, I'd like you to substitute the time you normally spend watching the news, reading a newspaper, and trawling Facebook with walking around your neighborhood. Don't even think about taking your phone. This is between you and Big Momma Nature.

Observe everything and be open to the idea that the plants, trees, and animals in your neighborhood have something important to tell you. Be willing to hear their nonstop vibration that offers all sorts of valuable information.

Any other news (like, say, the recent famine in Africa) doesn't really matter to you during the time frame of this experiment. *But that's heartless*, I hear you saying.

Being in reverent communion with the natural world is actually a path with far more heart. In reality, there's not much you can do about the famine in Africa (except contribute worry and guilt to the universal energy), but there's a lot you can do about your immediate neighborhood. And once we all get back into harmony with the universal energy, ending those famines in Africa will be a snap.

Take time to really look at the people in your life. Watch them with full-bodied amazement. Pretend as if you're meeting them for the very first time.

Be present to the sunrise. To the sunset. And every precious moment in between. Listen to the birds. Be open to messages from your pets.

Pay close attention to the moon, and if somebody asks you the question I asked at the beginning of this chapter, be prepared with an answer.

Lab Report Sheet

The Corollary: The Nature vs. News Corollary

The Theory: A vibrating, pulsing field with mystical information is available if I pay attention.

The Question: Is it possible that I'm seeing and believing in features of life that have no real relevance? And that I'm missing life-changing wisdom and lessons because I'm focused on the wrong things? Is it possible that nature itself has a message for me?

The Hypothesis: The more I'm connected to natural cycles and rhythms, the more energy and bandwidth of joy are available to me.

Time Required: 72 hours

Today's Date: _____ **Time:** _____

Deadline for Receiving Answer: _____

The Approach: For the next three days, I'm going to ban the news media (and yes, Facebook) from my awareness. Instead, I will seek the news from the natural world as I go outside and walk in my neighborhood. I will actively seek and expect an important message.

Research Notes: _____

_____

_____

"Man [should spend] less time proving that he can outwit Nature and more time tasting her sweetness and respecting her seniority."

— E. B. White, American author

165

RAINING CATS AND BLOGS

Facts vs. Truth

*"Really, weren't these facts just placeholders
until the long view could really assert itself?"*
— DAVID LEVITHAN, AMERICAN AUTHOR

I'm a journalist, trained, degreed, the whole nine yards. In fact, I started my illustrious journalism career at the *Kansas City Star*, the same newspaper where Ernest Hemingway and Walt Disney commenced their road to fame.

The last few years, however, I've begun to alter my beliefs about "the facts" I'm sworn by my profession to seek. I'm not so sure that "just the facts, ma'am" is helpful anymore. In fact, these so-called facts create a negative energetic momentum that I no longer want to perpetuate.

The "facts" I now choose to report are that happiness is our birthright, that love is the only reality, and that the only reason "facts" sometimes look otherwise is because that's what we've spent so many years focusing upon. I now know that it's unproductive to talk about, report on, or give attention to anything I don't want. And anytime I don't feel joyful and at peace is because I'm giving attention to something that disagrees with my Source. To use the old radio analogy, I've tuned in to an "oldies station" that still believes in pain and suffering.

I'm now committed to bringing a different energy to the party. An energy of love, an energy that sees only beauty, an energy that recognizes the Truth (and there is such a thing as Truth with a capital *T*, which is different from "facts") in every person.

I believe that's what Jesus meant when he said, "Turn the other cheek." He wasn't suggesting that we should walk around with bruised cheeks and black eyes. He was saying that we should begin moving in a different direction, turn our cheeks, so to speak, to a higher, brighter, more pleasing reality.

"Facts" are simply habits of thought we've been thinking so long that they now seem normal. When we invest in them over and over again, we validate them. We create more of them. "Facts" fill in around those beliefs.

Quantum physics has proven that it's impossible to observe anything without affecting it. Sadly, we've been seeking (and therefore affecting) things that no longer serve us. We've been seeking "facts" that were perpetuated long before we evolved to the place where we realized we have the power to change them. And, yes, they've picked up quite a bit of momentum. But at any time, we can "turn the other cheek" and look in a different direction.

As for me, I'm turning my cheek toward joy, toward peace of mind, toward the idea that all of us can be free and abundant and living lives of insatiable well-being.

THE "IF YOU SAY SO" COROLLARY (*OR* YOUR WORDS ARE WANDS THAT SHAPE YOUR LIFE)

Meme: What I Say Doesn't Matter.
Besides, I'm Only Responding to What I See.

Worldview 2.0: I Will Bring Abundance
and Joy into My Life Once I
Stop Talking Smack about It.

*"Words [are] things of beauty, each like a magical
powder or potion that could be combined with
other words to create powerful spells."*
— DEAN KOONTZ, AMERICAN AUTHOR

The Premise

Last I checked, the Yellow Pages doesn't have an entry for "Prophets" like they probably would have back in biblical days. But if you want a glimpse into your future, listen to the words you use to describe yourself and your life. When you say things like "This is going to be a great day," or "Things always work out for me," you are using your words to prophesy a positive future.

However, most of us, instead of utilizing the magic potion of our words, throw them around carelessly like confetti at a party. As in:

- "It's flu-and-cold season. I'll probably get it."
- "I have tried every diet out there, and I still can't lose weight."
- "I'm such an idiot. What was I thinking?"

At this point, most of us have little control over the ticker tape of thoughts that run through our minds, but we can monitor the commentary that proceeds out of our mouths.

Will Bowen, a former Unity minister who passed out purple bracelets to his congregation, challenging them to go 21 days without complaining, said he was shocked by how often he uttered negativity. During the first week of his challenge to refrain from complaining, gossiping, or criticizing, his personal best was six hours. And he is a *trained* minister.

Eventually, Bowen completed the 21-day challenge (it took several months) and his story swept the world, landing him spots in *People* magazine (compliments of yours truly), on *Oprah*, and on the *Today* show. Hundreds of thousands took the www.acomplaintfreeworld.org challenge, eventually sharing with Bowen that reformatting their mental hard drive relieved them of chronic pain, healed relationships, improved careers, and made them overall happier people.

But like Bowen, they were surprised by how automatic and rote their conversations are. Someone asks how we are, and without even giving it any thought, we repeat, "Fine, thank you. How are you?" Someone tells us about her great-aunt Ethel getting pancreatic cancer and we say, "Oh, I'm so sorry. That's horrible."

And usually, at the same time we blurt out our learned responses, our brains rapidly leaf through the file of information we've stored thus far about pancreatic cancer or cancer in general or about our friend, totally unrelated, who has breast cancer. As I said, it's all automatic and rote.

Words Call in Victory or Defeat

"You can change your world by changing your words."
— JOEL OSTEEN, PASTOR OF HOUSTON'S LAKEWOOD CHURCH

When my sister was in grade school, she believed each person was given a certain allotment of words. She was very judicious with what she said, because she thought that once she used up her allotment, she'd either die or become mute, neither an outcome she desired. Luckily, she now knows that words, like telemarketers, are pretty much unlimited, but that care in selecting which ones to use is a skill from which we could all benefit.

Every morning, we get the chance to bless our day or curse it. We can use words to describe a situation, or we can use them to change a situation. For example, you can call all your besties to complain how your husband never compliments you, or you can tell the tale of when you first fell in love. Both true stories. Completely different energy.

To endlessly tell the tale of how he forgot your birthday or about your boss who doesn't appreciate you is like watching *Spider-Man 3* over and over. It wasn't very good the first time you saw it, and it won't get better if you watch it again.

Most of us are savvy enough not to rush to Netflix when our least favorite movies come out, so why do we insist on running repeats of the least favorite events in our lives? To continue rehashing things that didn't please us makes no sense. Replaying negative stories only adds energy to them and emits a frequency that attracts more events with similar frequencies. Especially when we could use our allotment of words to inspire, uplift, and encourage.

Just like it's important to head west if you're going to California, it's important to send your words out in the direction you'd like your life to go.

I Do Declare

"Some people daily chant, 'I ain't got no money,' and wonder why they don't have enough money. Others chant, 'I'm not worthy or good enough,' and wonder why they are discouraged and not able to have the relationship, career, and life they desire. People 'language' themselves into manifestations they really don't want."

— REV. DR. TERRY COLE-WHITTAKER,
AMERICAN MINISTER AND NEW THOUGHT AUTHOR

The universe wants you to prosper and be healthy. It wants to provide for your every need, but when you keep blathering on about "never getting any breaks" or the "downsliding economy," it has no choice but to match you frequency for frequency.

Just like you can't watch NBC when your remote control enters the signal for ABC, you'll never prosper if you keep moaning about your piteous life. You can't talk lack and poverty and expect an abundant life. You can't continue to harp about how bad everything is and expect it to get better.

The universe is like the order taker at McDonald's. If can't give you a Big Mac if you keep ordering an Egg McMuffin.

Here are a few selections on the menu of life:

- "I've gone as far as I can go."
- "I'll never break this addiction."
- "I'm not that talented."
- "I'm not qualified."
- "I'd be wasting my time to ask that girl out."
- "I am blessed."
- "The universe supplies all my needs."
- "I live in divine health."
- "There's more where that came from."
- "The universe is opening new doors for me."

When we get our words going in the right direction, obstacles clear out, things turn around, and life starts to work.

Tell It Like You Want It to Be

"Words can be like X-rays if you use them properly—they'll go through anything."

— ALDOUS HUXLEY, AUTHOR OF *BRAVE NEW WORLD*

I have a friend who shall not be named that regularly accuses me of being a pie-in-the-sky Pollyanna. She thinks talking only about the good and the beautiful is denying facts.

But here's my position. "Facts" are not that interesting. I much prefer discussing possibilities. Sure those studies, those government reports, those doctors' prognoses declare what she might call irrefutable "facts." But to me, they're nothing but a catapult for something better.

I believe the most important faculty we possess is our imagination, and that by aligning it with the field of infinite potentiality, we can create something so much better than "current facts." Harping on about "current facts" just calls in more of the same. To waste our time on "appearances" is denying the power we have to change things for the better. I would much rather deny "facts" than deny my own ability to imagine something better. My words are the seeds that plant the possibilities.

We can continue to focus on "what is" or "what appears to be," or we can focus on what we can better imagine. "What is" is simply what we've been focusing on. "What could be" is much more interesting. At least to me.

Those "facts" that my friend accuses me of denying are nothing but the harvest of the words of lack and problems we spoke up until now.

Getting Bucked Off the Horse Yet Again

"Some people have a way with words,
and other people . . . oh, uh, not have way."
— STEVE MARTIN, AMERICAN COMEDIAN

When I turned 50, I threw my hands in the air and basically decided that my life was over. My many years of being a tall, hot blonde were about to come screeching to a halt. Or at least that's what I kept telling everyone.

Having supported a friend who is older than I am through menopause, I knew good and well what was coming. My skin was going to wrinkle and shrivel up, my ovaries would do a disappearing act, and my emotions were about to compete with the Coney Island Cyclone for number of ups and downs. I was like Paul Revere, riding my "woe is me" horse through the night, "Menopause is coming. Menopause is coming."

One day, while rigorously going through yet another book on how to cope with this horrible affliction, I finally got it. I am prophesying the future with my words and expectations. With my insistence on looking for signs of impending doom, my repeated chants of "Is it me? Or is it hot in here?" were paving the way for a difficult transition into a new phase of life. Even the name of this very natural cycle of life (crone, anyone?) lays a stone in the road ahead.

I snapped the cover of that book closed, called my friend, and said, "Thanks for loaning me that book on the symptoms of menopause, but I'm coming over right now to return it."

From that point on (except those times, yes, Taz, when I did get bucked out of the saddle), I began to declare and still declare to anyone who will listen:

- "Girl, you are looking so good today."
- "My best days are ahead of me."
- "I'm getting stronger and younger looking every day."
- "Health is flowing through me like the River Jordan."

Joel Osteen tells the story of a high school buddy of his. This guy was the star of the football team. He had thick, curly hair. He was what we girls used to call "a real hunk." Every time Joel asked him what he was up to, he'd say, "Oh, not much. Just getting old and fat and bald."

"I must have heard him say that 500 times," Joel recounts. "I hadn't seen him in 15, 20 years and ran into him the other day. And you know what? He ended up being a whiz at predicting the future. He was old and fat and bald."

If we continue to proclaim that we're tired and run-down, that we don't have any energy, we can certainly create that particular reality.

But instead of complaining, isn't it wiser to proclaim, "I am strong. I am full of energy. My vitality is being renewed"? The more we talk about being tired, the more tired we become. The more we persist in telling everyone how depressed we are, the more depressed we get. The more we talk about being overweight and out of shape, the more . . . well, I don't even want to say it.

Don't talk about the way you are. Talk about the way you want to be.

Louise Hay, my mentor, my publisher, and the most awesome 87-year-old on the planet, goes so far as to declare victory out loud right into the mirror. Mirror work, in case you've never heard of it, is where rather than asking the mirror, mirror on the wall who's the fairest of them all, you look deep into your own eyes and tell the reflection in that bloody mirror that you are beautiful, fabulous, worthy, talented, creative, and all sorts of other truths that far out-trump being "fair."

My friend Rhonda told me she was watching Louise Hay and Cheryl Richardson give a lecture called "You Can Create an Exceptional Life." Louise, who touts mirror work on a daily basis, reached into her bra at one point, pulled out a tiny mirror, looked into it, and said, "Hey, good-looking. How's it going?"

Now, that's someone who walks her talk.

Anecdotal Evidence

"The game of life is a game of boomerangs. Our thoughts, deeds, and words return to us sooner or later with astounding accuracy."

— Florence Scovel Shinn, author of *The Game of Life and How to Play It*

If you saw the 1976 film *The Pink Panther Strikes Again*, you may remember the phrase repeated by Chief Inspector Charles Dreyfus. After getting more and more stressed at Clouseau's incompetence, Dreyfus finally seeks out psychiatric advice and is prescribed the repetition of this phrase:

"Every day and in every way, I am getting better and better."

Although it didn't work for Dreyfus, this mantra-like autosuggestion was popularized by Émile Coué (1857–1926), a French psychologist and pharmacist who successfully employed what we now call the placebo effect. Coué noticed that when he raved to customers about a medicine's great effectiveness, they got better. When he said nothing, the medicine's effects were less dramatic.

More than the medicine itself, it was the belief in a medicine's effectiveness that proved so beneficial. One biography of Coué claimed a success rate of 93 percent, having cured everything from kidney problems and memory loss to diabetes, migraines, and even a prolapsed uterus. The other 7 percent were reportedly too skeptical to believe that saying the phrase that Inspector Dreyfus used (it has been satirized often in popular culture, including in the first episode of *Boardwalk Empire*, Season 3, when fugitive Nelson Van Alden repeats it into a mirror) could cure them.

As Coué himself liked to say, "I have never cured anyone in my life. All I do is show people how they can cure themselves." Curing anything, he said, requires a change in subconscious thought, which happens by repeating words until the subconscious absorbs them. He was way ahead of the curve in knowing that any idea exclusively occupying the mind eventually turns into reality.

More Anecdotal Evidence

"Call the things that are not, as though they were."
— ROMANS 4:16

In 1999, José Lima, the flamboyant pitcher from the Dominican Republic, had a fabulous season with the Houston Astros. He won 21 games and pitched in the All-Star Game. But in 2000, when the Astros debuted their new ballpark, he walked onto the diamond, took one look at the fence in left field that was a lot closer to home plate than the fence at the Astrodome, and said, "I'll never be able to pitch in here."

It ended up being a self-fulfilling prophecy. Despite the fans' enthusiasm for the new stadium, Lima plummeted from 21 wins to 16 losses. Never in the Astros history had a pitcher suffered such a profound negative turnaround.

I heard that story from Joel Osteen, head honcho at Lakewood Ministry in Houston. When Osteen took over the ministry after his father's death, he was scared and nervous. He thought, *I can't speak in public.*

But he knew better than to speak it aloud. Instead, he affirmed over and over again that the church's national TV audience would eat up his work. He even said these exact words about the now-popular Sunday morning show: "Once people turn me on, they just can't turn me off."

He got a letter the other day from a guy who said, "You know, Joel, I hate TV ministers. But my wife has been begging me to check out your show. I always put her off, tell her, 'Oh,

I will. I will.' But usually I just watch sports. One Sunday, I was fiddling around with the dials and the remote control got stuck on your show. I kept punching that button, kept trying to get back to the golf tournament I was watching. But for some reason, the remote wouldn't work. I even got up and put in some new batteries. Still wouldn't work. I finally just settled in and listened to you speak. And my wife was right. I like your show. But the funniest thing, as soon as your show was over, that remote started working just fine."

The Method

> *"If beating ourselves up worked,*
> *we'd all be thin, rich, and happy, wouldn't we?"*
> — CHERYL RICHARDSON, AMERICAN AUTHOR

If you've got screaming toddlers, I know you've used this phrase: "Honey, use your words."

And that's what we're going to do in this experiment.

We're going to use our words to call in the good, to declare favor over our lives, to place our faith in the unseen realm.

Here are the five steps:

1. Acknowledge that what you're noticing in your life now is only temporary unless you continue to cement it in day after day with your words.

2. For the next three days, for the time it takes to conduct this experiment, refrain from complaining. As Bob Marley used to say, a complaint is an invitation to the devil.

3. Say out loud: "Thank you for this fabulous day. I love _____ and I love _____." You can fill in the blanks with darned near anything,

because love emits a special frequency that can pierce the darkest of situations.

4. Last, you're going to pick a statement that you've been repeating for years: "My back's been hurting," or "I'm not good on first dates." Pick something your friends would recognize immediately, a familiar statement from your regular repertoire. Now, play the opposite game. Tell a completely different story for the next three days. Milk it for all you're worth. Act like you're Meryl Streep.

5. Look for evidence during the next 72 hours of this opposite reality.

Lab Report Sheet

The Corollary: The "If You Say So" Corollary

The Theory: The words that spill from my mouth have a certain wattage and energy, and by using only words and phrases that bless and uplift, I will empower myself and others.

The Question: Is it possible to positively affect my life by changing my conversations?

The Hypothesis: By actively monitoring my words, I will notice a change in what shows up in my life.

Time Required: 72 hours

Today's Date: _____ **Time:** _____

The Approach: For the next 72 hours, I'm going to refrain from rushing to react in speech until I've thought about each comment I make, ensuring that it passes the Quality Control requirements I've set up for myself. If during these three days I am successful in issuing no complaints, no wisecracks or unkind words about myself or others, I will feel a higher energy and notice a better-feeling vibration emanating from me.

Research Notes: _____

_____

_____

"Let us celebrate the occasion with wine and sweet words."

— PLAUTUS, ROMAN PLAYWRIGHT

RAINING CATS AND BLOGS

What *The Hangover Part III* Taught Me about Quantum Physics

"There's a certain delusional quality that all successful people have to have . . . you have to believe that something different can happen."
— WILL SMITH, AMERICAN ACTOR

Okay, true confession. I didn't see *The Hangover Part III*. Didn't even see the second in the trilogy.

But what this one-star summer bomb demonstrates is our tendency to repeat ourselves again and again, day after day. We get stuck in these loops, looking for the same things we saw yesterday. Today is a brand-new day with an infinite number of new possibilities.

Whoever took over for Ed McMahon could knock on your door with the winning check in the magazine sweepstakes. You could make a new friend or meet a potential S.O. You could get an idea for a book or a song or a nonprofit that might change the lives of millions.

The thing is, you never know. But because we get up every morning expecting the exact same thing, we get reruns (*Hangover Part III*'s) of yesterday. Yeah, there might be a little variety. You could get a speeding ticket, for example, or eat a pepperoni pizza instead of pasta, but admit it: You basically expect your world to look like a clone of yesterday.

But what if you woke up to a world where everything was completely unrecognizable? Are you willing to allow that possibility? The possibility that the world's largesse could flow into your life? The possibility that we could have peace on Earth? And that all children could go to bed with a full stomach knowing they were deeply loved and cherished?

If there's one thing I know, it's this: We get out of life exactly what we look for . . . down to the precise shape, size, and color.

A major conundrum of quantum physics is that whatever the observer expects to see, he sees. Physical reality, at its essence, is made of high-energy photons. And we, you and me, are patterns of light and information, patterns of light and information that we keep rerunning and rerunning.

So, to my way of thinking, the more open we are to brand-new, completely different possibilities, the better our world will become.

So, yeah, the first *Hangover* was kinda fun. But as for me, I'd rather see Bradley Cooper, Zach Galifianakis, and all those other actors starring in a whole new film.

EXPERIMENT #8

THE PLACEBO COROLLARY (*OR* THE TRUTH ABOUT BENDING REALITY)

Meme: Poor Me, a Separate, Pitiful Human Being Jostled Around by an Uncaring World.

Worldview 2.0: Reality Is Fluid and Constantly Changing, Reflecting Back My Innermost Beliefs.

*"We can never perceive what is real.
We can only perceive what is real for us."*
— BARBARA DEWEY, AUTHOR OF *AS YOU BELIEVE*

The Premise

This experiment will prove that your beliefs and expectations are powerful and profound. Indeed, they are the animating energy of life itself.

Your beliefs re-create and reproduce themselves in physical reality. Which is why thoughts become things. Why what you focus upon expands. The external world is the display screen of your innermost beliefs. These beliefs and expectations animate, sustain, and motivate all that you see. Blaming life for your misfortunes is like accusing your smartphone of running lousy apps. You're the one who downloaded them. Life simply serves as the projector of your beliefs and expectations.

Few of us truly understand the potency of our thoughts and consciousness. Each thought is a seed, a unit of mental energy. Those that carry sufficient intent, emotional impact, and conviction of belief (whether true or not) take root and stimulate materialization.

You might want to read that last bit again. Beliefs (whether true or not) stimulate materialization. So if you believe that life is an unending struggle, that bodies have no choice but to deteriorate, or that most guys are jerks, that's the script that will play out in your life.

Life itself is never painful. It is only a mirror of your beliefs. And just like you don't look in the mirror, notice your mascara is smudged, and then try to "fix it" on the mirror itself, you can't really "fix" your problems out there. You "fix" your problems by recognizing them as a case of mistaken identity and then changing the inner belief, the inner cause.

Where we get stuck is putting so much faith in a particular belief (*But it's true I have no money . . . It's true that I have cancer in my genetics*) that we cannot conceive that it's not fact. We're convinced it's "God's own gospel truth."

Facts, despite what scientists, teachers, and CNN tell you, are opinions, holding down material reality until we can move beyond.

Life as an Oversize Cartoon

"The function of the mind is to create coherence between our beliefs and the reality we experience."
— BRUCE LIPTON, PH.D., AUTHOR OF *THE BIOLOGY OF BELIEF*

Instead of using our thoughts and consciousness to imagine, expand, and create, we use this luminous superpower of an ability to run the data we downloaded from our culture, the data covering up and obscuring the powerful, magical now. Every atom, every molecule, every energy wave of your being pulses with creative life force. But instead of using this powerful mojo to generate brilliance, we turn it against ourselves.

I call it the Baby Huey principle. Baby Huey, a popular cartoon character when I was growing up, is a naïve, oversize duckling in diapers. Because he had the mentality of a baby but the size and strength of a sumo wrestler, he constantly caused problems, inadvertently knocking things over and damaging property. He had no idea of his superhuman strength. That's us, in a nutshell.

Our consciousness has the size and strength of a sumo wrestler, but because we don't know it, we squander this ability, making a mess of things. The only reason the world "stays" the way it is now is because we use our immense Baby Huey ability to stare at things we don't like. When we analyze and attempt to annihilate our seeming "problems," we clog up the pipes, scramble the energy flow.

The minute we withdraw our judgments, we get an empty, open moment where the field of infinite potentiality can arise.

Everybody Trance Now

"You spend your whole life stuck in the labyrinth, thinking about how you'll escape it one day. You just use the future to escape the present."
— JOHN GREEN, AUTHOR OF *THE FAULT IN OUR STARS*

Our beliefs about the way the world works serve as lightning rods, drawing into our experience "proof" that these "beliefs" are indeed hard and cold facts.

The problem, as I mentioned, is this animating energy cannot distinguish between what is fact and what is imagined to be fact. Beliefs, whether supplied by us or by our culture's dominant paradigm, reproduce themselves in physical form.

Hypnosis provides a good example. A hypnotist can tell his subject that an ice cube is a burning ember, and it will raise blisters. Or he can say a notebook is too heavy to lift, and no matter how hard his hypnotized subject tries, he will be unable to lift the flimsy notebook off the table. If the hypnotist informs his subject that he just ate a bag of Big Macs, his blood chemistry will reflect that statement.

In Michael Talbot's epic work *The Holographic Universe*, he tells the story of a guy named Tom who, after being hypnotized, was told his daughter Laura would be invisible when he came out of the trance. Even though Laura was standing directly in front of him and even giggled at the grand theater of it all, Tom could not see or hear her. The hypnotist then pulled a watch out of his pocket, held it against the small of Laura's back, and asked Tom if he could see what was in his hand. Tom leaned forward, stared right through his daughter, and not only was able to identify it as a pocket watch but could also read its inscription.

This challenges everything we "believe" about solid matter. It also indicates that what we see and experience may be nothing more than a collective decision—a sort of mass hypnosis.

More Than a Little White Pill

"Our thoughts hold more medicine than many of the astonishing breakthroughs of our time."

— KRIS CARR, AUTHOR OF *CRAZY SEXY KITCHEN*

Our beliefs and expectations, in fact, are so powerful that placebos (fake treatments like sugar pills, saline injections, and sham surgery) cause bald men to grow hair, high blood pressure to drop, ulcers to heal, dopamine levels to increase, and even tumors to shrink. And although pharmaceutical companies would rather keep this on the down low, placebos relieve symptoms on par with real medication.

In other words, it's our beliefs that do the healing.

Perhaps even more mind-stretching is the nocebo effect, the placebo's nefarious evil twin where dark expectations breed dark realities.

In one clinical drug trial after another, people report side effects they are warned about even when their test drug is a placebo. In one study on fibromyalgia, a full 11 percent of placebo takers dropped out due to debilitating side effects. Their thoughts created the symptoms.

After the 1995 nerve-gas attack in Tokyo, hospitals were flooded with patients suffering from nausea, dizziness, and other highly publicized symptoms even when they'd not been exposed. After a teacher at a Tennessee high school reported a gasoline smell and dizziness, the school was evacuated and around 100 students were rushed to the emergency room, 38 of whom were hospitalized overnight. An extensive investigation at the school discovered no chemicals, no gasoline, and no discernible reason for the symptoms—except expectation and belief.

Placebos, of course, are inert, but their effects are so real, creating even biochemical changes in the body, that it makes you wonder—or it should—how "factual" facts really are.

Mind Over Milk Shake

"I don't think we've given enough credit to the role of our beliefs in determining our physiology, our reality."
— ALIA CRUM, CLINICAL PSYCHOLOGIST AT COLUMBIA BUSINESS SCHOOL

NPR ran a fascinating story in May 2014 that demonstrated how powerfully our beliefs affect our physiology. Clinical psychologist Alia Crum concocted a supersize batch of French vanilla milk shake and put half in bottles labeled as a low-calorie drink (Sensishake) with zero fat, zero sugar, and a mere 140 calories. The other half (Indulgence) had labels indicating it was high in sugar and fat and had 620 calories. In truth, the drink had about 300 calories.

Before and after drinking the shakes, the test subjects were measured for a hormone called ghrelin. Doctors call it the "hunger hormone" because it's secreted in the gut and signals your body when it's time to eat. It also slows your metabolism, in the event you're not successful in your quest for nourishment. After you eat, ghrelin levels drop, which in turns signals the body that you're full and it's time to rev up the metabolism.

Crum, who has long studied the placebo effect, found that ghrelin levels dropped three times more for those who *thought* they were drinking a fatty shake than for those who believed their shake was the pinnacle of health. Clearly, she says, "Our beliefs matter in virtually every domain, in everything we do. Labels are not just labels. They evoke a set of beliefs. What we think is true becomes true for us."

And it works for more than your diet. Just thinking you got a great night's sleep makes you function better. One study reported in the *Journal of Experimental Psychology* hooked 164 students to equipment that supposedly showed how much time they spend in REM sleep, the high-quality stuff that makes you feel rested. One group was told they'd gotten above-average sleep, the other that they'd slept fitfully and not gotten their daily dose of REM. The two groups were given a test. Regardless of how well they slept (and no one really knows, because the machine was a sham and did nothing), those who believed they slept well outperformed the "tired" group.

Moral of this story? Even if you don't get enough sleep, you do yourself a grave disservice by whining about how tired you are.

Another study found that a group of hotel maids, in one month, lost weight, lowered their blood pressure, and improved their body fat percentages after being told their job provided a complete physical workout and met daily exercise guidelines. The control group was told nothing of the sort and, alas, lost no weight, nor dropped in blood pressure or body fat.

Anecdotal Evidence

*"It is not our physical state that limits us.
It is our mind-set about our own limits, our
perceptions, that draws the lines in the sand."*
— DR. ELLEN LANGER, HARVARD PROFESSOR OF PSYCHOLOGY

In 1981, Ellen Langer and her Harvard colleagues piled two groups of elderly men into vans, drove them to a monastery in New Hampshire, and told them to make-believe it was 1959. Her subjects, all in their 70s and 80s, were aided in their pretend game of being young again by mementos from that time period. Scattered throughout the rooms were old issues of *Life* magazine and *Saturday Evening Post*, a black-and-white television, a vintage radio. The men talked about Mickey Mantle, the launch of the first U.S. satellite, Castro's victory ride into Havana, Nikita Khrushchev and the need for bomb shelters. They even screened Jimmy Stewart's 1959 *Anatomy of a Murder.*

A battery of cognitive and physical tests was given before and after the week of pretend yesteryear. The results were so dramatic that even Langer, already suspicious that fixed ideas affect how we age, was shocked by the results.

Across the board, Langer's elderly test subjects showed improvement in height, weight, gait, posture, hearing, vision, and even performance on intelligence tests. Their joints were more flexible, their shoulders wider, their fingers more agile and less gnarled by arthritis.

"Wherever you put the mind, the body will follow," Langer said. "At the end of the study, I was playing football with these men, some of whom gave up their canes."

The Method

> *"The subconscious is not concerned with the truth or falsity of your feeling. It always accepts as true that which you feel to be true."*
>
> — NEVILLE GODDARD, BARBADIAN NEW THOUGHT PIONEER

In this experiment, you're going to create your very own placebo.

First, think of a physical issue you'd like to alter in some way. Maybe you get headaches. Or you have trouble sleeping. Maybe your stomach growls. Or you'd like to drop a pound or two. Or get rid of the bags under your eyes.

For the sake of the experiment, it's best to pick something physical (because it's easier to document), but the placebo effect works equally well on emotional issues. In fact, I would argue that physical issues, if you really break it down, are emotional issues in disguise. But, in the interest of scientific inquiry, we're looking for something physical to identify and document.

Now, pour a glass of water, rub your hands together to generate heat and energy, and hold them over the glass for 15 seconds. Voilà! Your cure.

Drink it slowly, concentrating on its healing effects. Pretend your doctor (or some other authority figure) wrote it out on a prescription pad.

Repeat for three days.

And remember what Harvard researcher Ellen Langer has proven in countless studies: It's not the placebo that affects recovery; it's the mind-set you adopt. In her words, *"You're making yourself better."*

Lab Report Sheet

The Corollary: The Placebo Corollary

The Theory: My thoughts are insanely powerful. So powerful I can flip reality by withdrawing my attention and shifting it to a different reality.

The Question: Is it possible I can concoct my own placebo?

The Hypothesis: If I spend three days drinking self-created, energy-infused water, I can improve or heal _____.

Time Required: 72 hours

Today's Date: _____ **Time:** _____

Date for Checking Results: _____

The Approach: Sounds crazy, but I will create my own placebo, drink it for three days straight, and see if I can accomplish the physical change I desire.

Research Notes: _____

_____

_____

*"The brain constructs a world based
on how you expect it to look."*

— BARBARA FREDRICKSON, AMERICAN PROFESSOR OF PSYCHOLOGY

Raining Cats and Blogs

The Anatomy of an Illness, aka the Ego's Secret Weapon

"A sick thought can devour the body's flesh more than fever or consumption."
— Guy de Maupassant, French writer

You might have heard that the American Psychiatric Association came out with a new manual this year for diagnosing mental illness. It's called the *Diagnostic and Statistical Manual of Mental Disorders V* (DSM-V), and you probably won't be surprised to learn that there are a number of new "diseases" in this fifth edition. The first DSM, which came out in 1952, listed 26 general disorders. Today, there are more than 400.

I'm not here to debate whether we're 16 times crazier today, but I have observed that illness (of all kinds) usually starts in the mind and goes from there. Advertisers know this. In fact, Steven Pressfield, author of one of my favorite books (*The War of Art*), said that his boss at a Madison Avenue ad agency instructed him to invent a disease, because "then we can sell the hell out of its cure."

According to *A Course in Miracles*, my main spiritual practice, our physical bodies are potent tools used by the ego for obscuring Truth, for hiding the body's inherent natural healing power.

Here's how it works:

1. You notice something's off.

2. You begin focusing on it.

3. You wonder what "it" might be (as opposed to knowing this Truth—that you are a child of the most high and cannot inherit illness).

4. You begin investing in it.

5. You give it a name.

6. You Google it, you start telling your friends about it, you join a support group.

Jill Bolte Taylor, a Harvard-trained neuroanatomist who studies the brain and became famous for her TED Talk, "My Stroke of Insight," says that an unresisted thought passes through the brain in 90 seconds.

That is, unless you decide to apply the above six steps.

Just saying . . .

EXPERIMENT #9

THE YABBA-DABBA-DOO COROLLARY (*OR* TRANSCENDENCE: IT'S JUST HOW WE ROLL)

Meme: Life Sucks and Then You Die.

Worldview 2.0: Life Is Miraculous,
and I Can't Really Die.

"Thinking that this physical world is all that matters is like shutting oneself up in a small closet and imagining that there is nothing else out beyond it."

— EBEN ALEXANDER, AMERICAN NEUROSURGEON
AND AUTHOR OF *PROOF OF HEAVEN*

E³

The Premise

My favorite cartoon, as a kid, was *The Flintstones*. No matter how many times I saw Dino outsmart Fred, I always chuckled when he got locked out of his cave house. I loved yelling "Wilmaaa!" right along with him.

I named this corollary after my favorite barefoot caveman—or rather after his well-known catchphrase—because in this experiment, we're going to ask for a glimpse of the other side, the inner sanctum. We're going to surrender to the Truth that we keep hearing is possible, but so often feel locked away from.

In the next 72 hours, you're going to knock, like Fred Flintstone, on the door, trusting that for at least a moment, you'll get an undistracted peek at the unfathomable Truth of who you really are and what life is.

Most of us experience life as a funhouse mirror, distorted and illusory, unaware of the intensely alive energy field that surrounds and flows through us like a gushing river. This field, this ongoing Divine Broadcast of love, is available 24-7 and wants to be known and expressed through us. It's the bedrock (pardon the pun) of who we are, of what is possible.

And here's the deal. We only *think* we're locked out. We're outside yelling "Wilmaaa!" because we view life through the lens of our fears, through the mental constructs we've erected. We act out of our compulsive beliefs, behaviors, and ongoing resistance to life itself. Our consciousness is rerunning yesterday's *Flintstones* episode.

But like Fred, we're the idiots who locked ourselves out. We're the ones who cut ourselves off from the sustenance and never-ending love that is as near as the air we breathe.

This Truth, this radiant X, can direct us, can heal us, and can provide for our every necessity. We only need surrender and open the door.

Tweak and Ye Shall Find

*"Get yourself in alignment with the
quantum field and you'll beam like the sun."*
—RUSSELL BRAND, RABBLE-ROUSING BRITISH ACTOR

Let's eat, Grandma!
Let's eat Grandma!

There's but one comma's difference in the two sentences above, but they're as different as a Hallmark commercial and a cannibal.

And that's what this section is about: tweaking the little things, moving your energetic vibration just a tad bit closer to the majestic field of infinite potentiality. The FP has no limits and answers to none of the physical laws we do, so the best tool in our Batman utility belt is to get our thoughts, emotions, and consciousness aligned with the FP.

When our vibration or energetic frequency is clear, open, and loving, life unfolds effortlessly. When we operate from a distorted frequency, we encounter snags, snarls, and snafus at every turn. Although most of us have trained ourselves *not* to see energy or anything else that's culturally impermissible, if we *could* see it, we'd quickly realize that what we call "a problem"—be it a problem with our health, relationships, or finances—is nothing but blocked energy.

Our energetic vibration acts as a filter, a set of instructions that either green-lights our good or deters it as something "out there." Once we tune in to a clear, happy frequency, life becomes magical, miraculous even.

And despite what Worldview 1.0 teaches, upgrading your frequency is far more effective than physical effort at influencing the material world. It's not some feel-good woo-woo either, although you will feel a gazillion times better as you slide into alignment home plate. It's based on the tenets—although not yet quite understood—of quantum physics.

199

One degree—one tiny degree—is all it takes for an airline pilot to miss his landing target. Stray just one degree from your flight pattern for one measly mile and you'll land 92 feet away from your target. Keep that one degree going for 60 miles and you'll land an entire mile from your intended target. On a flight between LAX and JFK, that one seemingly insignificant degree would mean an EPA (estimated *place* of arrival) of 40 miles out in the freezing-cold Atlantic.

So when I insisted on changing the wording in the contract for this book from *if* sales reach a certain number to *when* sales reach a certain number, I was tweaking my future. If you listen to yourself and others, even those who are complete disciples of the law of attraction, you'll notice all kinds of words that aren't sailing in the direction of your intention.

Call it quibbling, but these small, correctable patterns of thought and speech can quickly get you back on course. It doesn't take much (what's one simple word?), but the impact on your life is huge.

M&Ms, or Miracle Mind-sets

"When we take one step, the universe takes 10,000."
— MIKE DOOLEY, CREATOR OF *NOTES FROM THE UNIVERSE*

TWEAK #1: I "have to" vs. I "get to." Instead of thinking you *have* to do something, it's always wise to realize you *get the opportunity* to do whatever it is. That tiny tweak in wording (I *get* to go to my job, I *get* to have this uncomfortable conversation with my wife, I *get* to hear my lab results today) is often enough to reroute the flight pattern of your life.

I've heard this ugly rumor that there are people out there who don't like their jobs. People who don't get excited when

"The End" rolls on the screen of their weekend. I've even heard more heart attacks happen on Monday (again something to do with work) than any other day of the week.

Since my *work* today (that word never really cuts it for me, because, as you know, I. Love. Everything. About. My. Job.) is offering tweaks, I'd like to suggest this sentiment: T.G.I.M.

Start Monday with this: *I am so excited I get to go back to making money today.*

Tweak #2: "It's just the way it is" vs. "What else is possible?" Once you loosen the rules and let go of all those "facts" you learned in school, all the patterns you picked up from your family and culture, you begin to see a whole different reality. The only reason your life looks the same today as it did yesterday is because that's where you've invested your energy. You're stuck in habitual patterns of perception. You miss all kinds of miracles because you focus only on what is "known."

Instead of focusing on what's the same, on what's familiar, ask, *What else is new?* Playing make-believe, as we did as children, is a much holier tack. In fact, what we see and believe as "reality" now is simply what we're currently "making believe" is true.

Instead of "telling it like it is," ask questions like these:

- "What might happen in the next moment?"
- "What is possible if I let go of everything I know?"
- "How would life be if I surrendered all my beliefs?"
- "What if everything is absolutely perfect?"

As Richard Bartlett, author of *Matrix Energetics,* says, "When we change our consciousness around what is possible, rather than being limited by a reality construct dominated by what isn't possible, we discover that we are actually able to employ quantum energies and principles in our day-to-day lives in unexpected, fun—and miraculous—ways."

Tweak #3: "Why can't I do this?" vs. "What if?" When you ask "Why can't I do this?" you obtain useless data. When you ask different questions, apply a different reference frame, you get different—and I would suggest better—information.

Cultivating the habit of asking powerful, open-ended questions trains your right brain to listen to signals from your subconscious. Here are some of my "what-if" questions that you're welcome to borrow:

- "What if cancer could be healed instantly?"
- "What if I wake up tomorrow and look younger?"
- "What if life can keep getting better and better?"
- "What if I start each day with a completely clear slate?"

It's like a deck of cards. Pick a reality, any reality.

Tweak #4: "There's not enough" vs. "There's more where that came from." Most of us have a tendency to believe in limits. Instead of realizing the infinity of our Source, we put the brakes on and worry there's only so much to go around.

When my friend Carla's four kids were young, she used to constantly think, *There's never enough time.* After several years of creating that reality, she got it.

She began affirming, "There is always plenty of time."

"It was the funniest thing," she says. "The days still had the same 24 hours, but everything changed. I suddenly had exactly what I had called in: plenty of time."

TWEAK #5: "It's hard" vs. "It's a piece of cake." There's a four-letter word that, as far as I'm concerned, is one of the most dangerous words in the English language. It's especially damning when combined with something you hope to accomplish, such as lose weight, attract money, get a hot date.

The word is *hard,* as in "It is hard to _____" (pick your poison). Because our beliefs are so powerful, literally sculpting our lives on a moment-by-moment basis, to believe (and especially to say out loud) that anything is difficult is extremely counterproductive. If we expect things to be hard, we can certainly create life that way. As for me, I prefer creating a life where I simply open the doors and windows and let Source and all its accompanying blessings flow freely in.

My beautiful colleague and friend Annola Charity presented me with a Staples "Easy" button. This three-inch red button, when pressed, repeats, "That was easy." It's now one of my mantras. I affirm that the more I hand over to the universe (the field of infinite potentiality that is *so* much smarter than I am), the better my life becomes.

TWEAK #6: "I'm all alone" vs. "I am connected to everything." Potentially, you are in touch with every person, every answer, every material thing you could ever want. Absolutely everything is available to you. It's impossible to cut yourself off from this connection. Can you imagine one Christmas light in a string of lights complaining, "I'm not glowing over here. What's wrong with me? Why am I separate? Why am I cut off? How do I fix this big problem?"

You fix the problem by giving up the belief you have a problem. You are hooked forever and for all time to the FP and everything else you desire.

So if you want to "manifest" something, simply begin to put your attention on it. Whatever you put your attention on comes alive, like those kids' computer games. When you point your cursor on, say, a cupboard, the door opens and a mouse starts dancing or a ball starts bouncing.

If you put your cursor on all the opportunities and love in the scenes of your life, that reality comes alive. But if you continue to click on the monsters under the bed, they, too, are more than happy to put in an appearance. The thing is we're the ones manning the dials. We're the ones deciding where to point our cursors, where to send our attention.

Anecdotal Evidence

Contestant Number 43,212

*"We have nothing to lose by attempting
to achieve the miraculous."*
— Bernie Siegel, American physician and
author of *A Book of Miracles*

If you're one of the five people on planet Earth who hasn't yet heard of Susan Boyle, allow me the pleasure of introducing you. This Scottish mezzo-soprano, whom comedian Stephen Colbert described at the Grammys as "a 48-year-old cat lady in sensible shoes," is the quintessential model of transcendence.

She was the youngest of nine kids. Her dad was a miner. The family got by, barely. When she was born on April 1, 1961, there was trouble with her delivery, and doctors told her parents that because of a sustained absence of oxygen, she was probably going to be a slow learner, lead a second-rate life. At school, she was bullied, called "Susie Simple."

She had one short-lived job as a cook's apprentice and lived at home with her parents until her dad and then her mom finally passed in 2007 when Susan was 46. A year later, still grieving, Susan Magdalene Boyle showed up for an audition on *Britain's Got Talent.* She was decades older than most of the contestants, certainly a lot less "hip." She had a thick accent and looked about as opposite as you can get from most successful singers today.

Until she headed to Glasgow for that now-famous audition, she had never sung for an audience bigger than her parish church, had never even ridden a bus by herself. In fact, when departing her hometown of Blackburn, Scotland, she initially boarded the wrong bus.

When she stepped out onto the stage, barely getting a bored glance from Simon Cowell and the other judges, she looked like the rest of us: average, scared, and destined to be forgotten.

But before she could even finish her captivating performance of "I Dreamed a Dream" from *Les Misérables,* the entire audience was standing, applauding wildly, and Simon Cowell was, for once, speechless.

Within nine days, her audition had been watched by 100 million YouTube viewers, and when her album debuted a few months later, it was the best-selling album across the globe, knocking out Leona Lewis's *Spirit* as the U.K.'s best-selling debut album of all time.

SuBo (as the media began to call this Scottish songstress with the big voice) has since gone on to sing for the Queen of England, Oprah, and Pope Benedict. She has performed with her idols, Donny Osmond and Elaine Paige, and less than a year after that transcendent performance, was voted by *Time* magazine as the seventh-most-influential person in the world.

Needless to say, she no longer lives in poverty.

So no matter how long you've been locked out or how average you may feel, it's completely irrelevant. It matters not one whit what the doctors said, the names your classmates called you, or what career you might have had or not had. It doesn't even matter whether you initially got on the wrong bus. Or that you don't feel as hip or as young as everybody else.

Your transcendence is inevitable. Your connection to the FP is as sure as tomorrow's sunrise.

The Method

> *"The way is not hard, but it is very different."*
> — *A Course in Miracles*

If you could shut down the ticker tape that continually runs on the edge of your consciousness, you wouldn't need this experiment. You'd be living in and continually aware of the Sacred Buzz, the Truth of your ever-expanding good.

Most of us, instead, believe we have to wait. We have to follow the proper steps. The stars have to be lined up. The balls with our lottery numbers have to drop. But it's here now, surrounding us, bathing us in peace, love, and joy.

This experiment is not about getting anything. It's about letting. Letting Truth be. To do this experiment properly, you have to let go of your fears. Set aside the erroneous notion that reality is frightening or not to your liking. More than a seeking of something, this experiment is akin to a blowtorch, blasting away everything that isn't real.

Here are the steps:

1. Ask the FP, sincerely and fervently, for a transcendent moment. Ask to be clearly shown. Although many have tried to explain transcendence (Kant, for example, called it "that which goes beyond"), it's so big and so extraordinary that words have little ability to illustrate it. Suffice it to say that when you get there, you will not miss it.

2. Every time you're in front of a mirror during the next three days (way too often, for most of us in the Western world), look deep into your eyes and repeat to yourself, "This is not who I really am. I am so much more than this limited body." This leaves some wiggle room in your reality.

3. Allow yourself the luxury of being absorbed in a feeling of being deeply loved, being taken care of, having the abundance of all you need. Sink down into this infinite care the way you'd sink into an overstuffed couch.

4. Whenever possible, notice the buzz within your body. As you take your attention off thought, you'll feel this buzzing of energy flowing through your body. I call it "The Big Happy."

5. As you start to detach from your over-amped mind, you'll notice a fluidity, an opening, a less-solid feeling, and drop down into a neutral, endless ocean of infinite possibilities.

Lab Report Sheet

The Corollary: The Yabba-dabba-doo Corollary

The Theory: There is an invisible energy force or field of infinite possibilities.

The Question: If there really is an invisible river of life, a force field that provides the blueprint for my life, why am I so often unaware of it? And is it possible that I can hook in to it?

The Hypothesis: If I release the resistance to that which is trying to come forth through me, I will get a glimpse, a sampling, of what life really is.

Time Required: 72 hours

Today's Date: _____ **Time:** _____

The Approach: Okay, FP, this is your moment of glory. I expect to be shown a glimpse of my connection to the field complete with the awe and the magnitude. I've heard that once it comes, there's no mistaking it. For the next 72 hours, I am going to be consciously receptive, listening and trusting that I will catch a glimpse of the river of life.

Research Notes: _____

_____

_____

*"Life is not a problem to be solved, but a
reality to be experienced."*

— Søren Kierkegaard, Danish philosopher

RAINING CATS AND BLOGS

It's TGIF, Boos

"Celebrate what you want to see more of."
— TOM PETERS, AUTHOR OF *IN SEARCH OF EXCELLENCE*

Time to get out and celebrate. Time to remember how lucky you are, time to give praise to the highest of holies. As my mentor Rob Brezsny would say, "Let's break open the forbidden happiness."

Sure, I have a to-do list. In fact, I have two of them.

On mine:

1. Dream up better questions.
2. Have the best day of my life.

The other to-do list is for Source, God, the field of infinite potentiality.

Here's what it says:

1. Handle everything else.

AFTERWORD

Bonus Experiment #10:
The Marriage at Cana Corollary
(*or* It's Time to Get D-O-W-N!)

"I do not believe in miracles, I rely on them."
— Yogi Bhajan, Indian guru

Woot-woot! You made it through the book. Which can only mean one thing. It's time to party rock. It's time to hoot and holler, throw out confetti, dance, and generally whoop it up!

I don't know about you, but in my world, a celebration this huge usually includes adult beverages.

And now that we're so *over* those antiquated, I'm-a-victim, I-have-no-power attitudes, I'm thinking it's time to turn some water into wine. Yep, this is the experiment for overachievers.

Before you get your knickers in a knot, let me just say that I am the first to admit it's pretty "out there." But I also know that until my consciousness can embrace a new possibility, it will remain beyond my purview. Just like the ability to run a four-minute mile was considered ridiculous nonsense until Roger Bannister finally did it on May 6, 1954 (and this feat has since been repeated many times), it's ridiculous nonsense to disciples of Worldview 1.0 that they have any say in miracles.

So I hereby invoke the four-minute-mile rule, the one that says that if one person did it, the rest of us can do it, too. Well, one person did it.

In John 2:11, Mary, being a typical Jewish mother, asks JC to intervene when the wedding hosts run out of wine. Although he's reluctant at first, he does what any good Jewish son does when his mom makes him feel guilty. He asks for six jugs of water (easy enough to get from the local well) and, by hooking into the field of infinite potentiality, transforms one reality (water) into a different reality. He changed the water's molecular composition into that of wine.

Had *Wine Spectator* been around back then, it would have, according to the overseer—who, of course, had to sample it—gotten a 99.9 rating. This wine was good.

I've heard rumors there are some fundamentalists out there who think JC actually turned those six jugs of water into grape juice, but, as for my party, I'm thinking only a nice glass of Cabernet will do.

Anecdotal Evidence

> *"I pray for the change in perception that will let me see bigger and sweeter realities."*
> — ANNE LAMOTT, AMERICAN NOVELIST AND PROGRESSIVE SPIRITUAL ACTIVIST

Qigong masters in China regularly alter the taste of brandy. Using qi energy, they're able to purify and refine brandy. Robert Peng, an internationally renowned qigong master who now lives in New York City, claims even beginners can perform this simple technique. He teaches it at workshops and writes about it in his book, *The Master Key: Qigong Secrets for Vitality, Love, and Wisdom.*

He recommends pouring two glasses to compare—which, he told me, end up tasting startlingly different. As he says, "If you can transform the taste of alcohol in under a minute using your own willpower, what do you suppose happens when you recycle hurtful thoughts about yourself? And what effect do you have on others as a result of negative projections? We are increasingly concerned about air pollution, water pollution, electronic pollution, and noise pollution, but how mindful are we about the 'pollution' caused by our own consciousness?"

He says the line between our private thoughts and the outer world is permeable and that our negative thoughts leave invisible "bloody fingerprints."

The Method

"A miracle is when one plus one equals a thousand."
— FREDERICK BUECHNER, AUTHOR OF *THE ALPHABET OF GRACE*

These steps are adapted from Robert Peng's Exercise 11 in "Mastering Willpower" from his book, *The Master Key.*

1. Pour water into a wineglass. Place it directly in front of you.

2. Rub your hands together vigorously for 20 seconds, then hold them about a foot apart on either side of the glass as you create a qi Field between your palms. Feel your energy penetrate the liquid inside the glass for 20 seconds.

3. Pick up the glass. Visualize a brilliant light shining down from your hand into the liquid

and beyond. Feel your energy flowing. Visualize the water turning into wine. Continue sending your energy for one full minute.

4. Imagine beams of golden energy shooting from your fingertips and use the qi to "stir" (sorry, Bond, James Bond) and refine. Feel your qi inside the glass transforming the water. Smile as you continue doing this in a steady and relaxed way for up to one minute.

5. With your index and middle finger, make what Peng calls "a blade of sword finger" and seal the energy in the glass.

6. Drink with unbridled glee!

Lab Report Sheet

The Corollary: The Marriage at Cana Corollary

The Theory: If one person did something, it's possible for all.

The Question: Is it possible to turn water into wine? If indeed Jesus did it, then can I do it, too?

The Hypothesis: If I put water into a wineglass, I can use qigong energy to turn it into wine.

Time Required: 3 minutes

Today's Date: _____ **Time:** _____

Deadline for Receiving Answer: _____

The Approach: I will follow the steps and visualize the end results of the big honking party I'm about to have.

Research Notes: <u>You'll notice I filled in this section for you, because who wants to be taking notes at a party? Shout-outs for sticking with me through the experiments, for being open-minded, and for helping me change the dominant paradigm. Whatever you do, don't stop now. Keep being courageous, keep exploring, and keep using these principles for a genuine exploration of untrodden ways. Now, would you get out there and drink some wine?!</u>

*"Without deviation from the
norm, progress is not possible."*

— Frank Zappa, American musician

ACKNOWLEDGMENTS

There are at least seven billion people* I'd like to thank. I feel so grateful to be living at this time when it really is possible that all of us could be fed and housed and living together peacefully.

Since I believe in saying "thank you" for what I most desire (doing so makes it come alive), I want to thank every single one of you for choosing to dance instead of fight, for choosing to love instead of judge, for choosing to open your heart instead of running away from what is now truly possible.

A few specific members of the seven billion merit a lot more than I could ever write on this page. But I'll try.

Shout-outs to:

- Reid Tracy, for making all this happen

- Louise and Wayne, for telling the world

- Alex Freemon, for being an editor most extraordinaire

- Jim Dick, for being patient and being a type F personality

- The whole Sheridan clan, who, added together, make up a sizable percentage of those seven billion

---

* The United Nation's last estimate of world population.

- Donna Abate, Diane Ray, Pam Homan, Stacey Smith, Perry Crowe, and all my other new Hay House friends

- My Vortex group

- My power posse (Linda Gwaltney, Carla Mumma, Annola Charity, Elizabeth Stiers, and Diane Silver), for faithfully joining me in daily awesomeness

- Spiritual entrepreneurs (you know who you are)

- Joyce Barrett, who has been meeting me for coffee and conversation for at least five years

- Rhonda Burgess, who always seems to know the perfect time to invite me for martinis

- Wendy Druen and Kitty Shea, who have always been my most faithful readers

- Betty Shaffer, my best *Course in Miracles* comrade

- All the readers of *E-Squared,* who made 2013 the best year of my life . . . so far!

- And my best buddy and pal, Tasman McKay Grout

ABOUT THE AUTHOR

Pam Grout is the #1 *New York Times* best-selling author of 17 books, three plays, a television series, and two iPhone apps. She writes for *People* magazine, CNN Travel, *The Huffington Post, Men's Journal,* and her luxury travel blog, www .georgeclooneyslepthere.com. She's also a devoted mom, pickleball player, and crossword-puzzle junkie.

Find out more about Pam and her out-of-the-box take on life on her sometimes-updated website: www.pamgrout .com.

Hay House Titles of Related Interest

YOU CAN HEAL YOUR LIFE, the movie, starring Louise Hay & Friends
(available as a 1-DVD program and an expanded 2-DVD set)
Watch the trailer at: www.LouiseHayMovie.com

THE SHIFT, the movie, starring Dr. Wayne W. Dyer
(available as a 1-DVD program and an expanded 2-DVD set)
Watch the trailer at: www.DyerMovie.com

DAILY LOVE: Growing into Grace, by Mastin Kipp

HOLY SHIFT!: 365 Daily Meditations from A Course in Miracles,
edited by Robert Holden, Ph.D.

THE MAP: Finding the Magic and Meaning in the Story of Your Life,
by Colette Baron-Reid

*MIRACLES NOW: 108 Life-Changing Tools for Less Stress, More Flow,
and Finding Your True Purpose,* by Gabrielle Bernstein

THE TOP TEN THINGS DEAD PEOPLE WANT TO TELL YOU,
by Mike Dooley

VIRUS OF THE MIND: The New Science of the Meme,
by Richard Brodie

YOU ARE THE PLACEBO: Making Your Mind Matter,
by Dr. Joe Dispenza

YOU CAN CREATE AN EXCEPTIONAL LIFE,
by Louise Hay and Cheryl Richardson

All of the above are available at your local bookstore,
or may be ordered by contacting Hay House (see next page).

We hope you enjoyed this Hay House book. If you'd like to receive our online catalog featuring additional information on Hay House books and products, or if you'd like to find out more about the Hay Foundation, please contact:

Hay House, Inc., P.O. Box 5100, Carlsbad, CA 92018-5100
(760) 431-7695 or (800) 654-5126
(760) 431-6948 (fax) or (800) 650-5115 (fax)
www.hayhouse.com® • www.hayfoundation.org

Published and distributed in Australia by: Hay House Australia Pty. Ltd.,
18/36 Ralph St., Alexandria NSW 2015
Phone: 612-9669-4299 • *Fax:* 612-9669-4144 • www.hayhouse.com.au

Published and distributed in the United Kingdom by: Hay House UK, Ltd.,
Astley House, 33 Notting Hill Gate, London W11 3JQ
Phone: 44-20-3675-2450 • *Fax:* 44-20-3675-2451 • www.hayhouse.co.uk

Published and distributed in the Republic of South Africa by:
Hay House SA (Pty), Ltd., P.O. Box 990, Witkoppen 2068
Phone/Fax: 27-11-467-8904 • www.hayhouse.co.za

Published in India by: Hay House Publishers India, Muskaan Complex,
Plot No. 3, B-2, Vasant Kunj, New Delhi 110 070
Phone: 91-11-4176-1620 • *Fax:* 91-11-4176-1630 • www.hayhouse.co.in

Distributed in Canada by: Raincoast Books,
2440 Viking Way, Richmond, B.C. V6V 1N2
Phone: 1-800-663-5714 • *Fax:* 1-800-565-3770 • www.raincoast.com

Take Your Soul on a Vacation

Visit www.HealYourLife.com® to regroup, recharge,
and reconnect with your own magnificence.
Featuring blogs, mind-body-spirit news, and
life-changing wisdom from Louise Hay and friends.

Visit www.HealYourLife.com today!